THE MORRIS ISLAND LIGHTHOUSE

THE
MORRIS ISLAND
LIGHTHOUSE

CHARLESTON'S MARITIME BEACON

DOUGLAS W. BOSTICK

FOREWORD BY RICHARD L. BECK, DMD,
CHAIRMAN, SAVE THE LIGHT, INC.

THE
History
PRESS

Published by The History Press
Charleston, SC 29403
www.historypress.net

Cover design by Marshall Hudson.
Cover image: The Morris Island Lighthouse. *Photo by Richard L. Beck, DMD, and chairman of Save the Light, Inc.*

First published 2008
Second printing 2013

ISBN 9781540218759

Library of Congress Cataloging-in-Publication Data

Bostick, Douglas W.
The Morris Island Lighthouse : Charleston's maritime beacon / Douglas W. Bostick.
p. cm.
Includes bibliographical references.
ISBN 978-1-59629-470-7
1. Morris Island Lighthouse (Folly Beach, S.C.)--History. I. Title.
VK1025.M67B68 2008
387.1'5509757915--dc22
2008009763

This book is dedicated to the members and board members of Save the Light. We all owe them a vote of thanks for accomplishing what everyone else said could not be done.

Contents

Foreword

The Morris Island Lighthouse is the most beloved reminder of South Carolina's maritime roots. It is the state's only first-order light station. This lighthouse and its two predecessors have welcomed and guided mariners safely to our shores for three centuries. This important book by Doug Bostick chronicles the history of our beloved lighthouse and the keepers and families who braved sometimes brutal conditions and meager provisions to ensure the safety of ships entering Charleston Harbor.

Sea Island and Charleston residents are hopeful that Long Island, located between James Island and Folly Beach, with its unmatched beauty and species diversity can be preserved in its natural state. Long Island, along with Black Island, held in trust by the Ohlandt family; the East end of Folly Island, held in trust by Charleston County Parks and Recreation Commission; and Morris Island, recently returned to the public domain, could form an important natural and cultural conservation region.

There are many reasons to love and preserve the Morris Island Lighthouse. So much a part of the fabric of our past, so much a reminder of our maritime roots and so beautiful as a gateway to the treasures of the natural beauty that bless this community, it is easy to understand why there is such strong support for Save the Light. Our mission is simply to preserve this historic icon for the people of South Carolina.

I trust you will find the many stories about Morris Island and the lighthouse fascinating and informative. May it lead to a greater appreciation of the rich historic treasures we are fortunate to still enjoy.

Richard L. Beck, DMD
Chairman, Save the Light, Inc.

Acknowledgements

I was raised on James Island, in the shadow of the Morris Island Lighthouse. As youths, my friends and I treated the lighthouse as a great mystery. We were drawn to it yet never could get to it. We imagined great stories about living on Morris Island and the devastation of the war years, and we tried to understand how an island disappears.

My grandmother spent many summers visiting her brother-in-law, a lightkeeper on Morris Island in the early twentieth century. She and my grandfather, Jack, were avid fishermen, going out in their boat most days of the week. Grandmother and Jack cast for their own bait, raked their own oysters and brought home plenty of fish. When other favorite fishing holes failed, they would head to the jetties. One of my favorite Saturday adventures was fishing with them in the daytime and then heading to their house for an oyster roast in the evening. Grandmother always warned us to never eat sweets after eating oysters. I always assumed she made that up since sweet desserts cannot be caught at the end of a hook.

My goals with this book were to share the many fascinating stories of the Morris Island Lighthouse and to peek into the lives of those who braved the isolation and bore the brunt of extreme weather in order to provide safe passage for the many ships finding their way to Charleston Harbor.

I am indebted to the staffs of the South Carolina Historical Society, the Charleston Library Society and the South Carolina Room of the Charleston County Public Library. Thank you to the patient staff at the National Archives, the Library of Congress and the office of the U.S. Coast Guard historian.

Thank you to my good friend Mrs. Roulain Deveaux, the granddaughter of Captain John Wieking, for sharing her stories and family photographs. I also want to offer my gratitude to Katherine Davis Craig, the daughter of lightkeeper W.A. Davis. Her pictures, taken with her Brownie camera, are a treasure trove.

Thank you to Save the Light chairman and photography enthusiast Richard Beck for the use of his many photographs. His never-ending passion for the preservation of the Morris Island Lighthouse is admirable and contagious. I am also indebted to Jim Booth for the use of his images and the opportunity to review his lighthouse files. He has kept us entranced for years with his stunning paintings of the lighthouse and historic sites in our beloved Lowcountry.

I appreciate the kind permission from the late Faith Ferguson, the granddaughter of Reverend Cornish, for use of her family photographs of Morris Island.

I want to convey my admiration and thanks to Barbara Schoch. She understood the need to preserve this iconic image of South Carolina's maritime history. When everyone said, "You can't!" she said, "I can and I will." Every great grass-roots effort has to start with someone; this one started with Barbara.

One often hears the expression, "They broke the mold with him!" Johnny Ohlandt would have *never* fit into a mold. He is the quintessential one of a kind. He has been the equivalent of the modern-day lightkeeper for the Morris Island Lighthouse.

My good friend Fred Wichmann has inspired me. Fred was born at the Cape Romain Lighthouse at McClellanville. An avid wooden boat fan, he has devoted himself to several local history projects, the lighthouse included.

Many of the Save the Light board members like Paula Hinton, Barry McLaurin, Robert New and Al Hitchcock have sustained a passionate devotion to the task of preserving this lighthouse for many, many years. There are also a number of professionals, most notably Jack Corgan and Carroll Crowther, who volunteered their technical and organizational expertise to the lighthouse preservation project. Theirs is the kind of effort and devotion that you could never get if you did pay for it. For them, the trip has been a labor of love.

Chris Nichols wrote a marvelous thesis in 2000, reviewing the cultural and shoreline changes on Morris Island. He has graciously allowed the use of his research and maps to assist this book.

Thank you to Magan Lyons, Jaime Muehl and Marshall Hudson for their encouragement and advice, making this a better project. I also offer my admiration to Kirsty Sutton and everyone at The History Press. Their work in preserving the great stories that are often lost in our local history is appreciated. Without these stories, we all lose our connection to our pasts.

Finally, as always, thank you to my family for their loving support and encouragement. Everything I do, I do to honor them. They teach me every day that the destination in our lives is not nearly as important as loving, appreciating and enjoying those with us on our journey through life.

First Light

The ninety-six passengers aboard the frigate *Carolina* were surely relieved and overjoyed as the ship eased into a natural harbor. They were part of an expedition to create an English settlement north of the Spanish settlements in Florida and south of Virginia.

On a beautiful April day in 1670, Captain Henry Brayne navigated through the islands guarding the entrance to this beautiful land. He continued past a point of land covered with oyster shells, clear evidence of a Native American presence. Now in the harbor, he navigated to the west and up a river he would later learn the local tribes called Kiawah. On the western bank of the river, Brayne spotted a navigable creek where he aimed his vessel for landing.

The trip from England had been an arduous journey. The *Carolina* was one of three ships in the expedition. Its passengers had been at sea for seven long months, leaving England in August 1669. After a short stop in Ireland, the expedition continued to the New World, reaching Barbados by October. During the lengthy and treacherous voyage, the other two ships had been lost, leaving the *Carolina* on a lonely quest to reach this new land full of promise.

On departure from England, the expedition had loaded all the necessary provisions to create a new English settlement:

> *15 tons of beer, 30 gallons of brandy, 59 bushels of flour, 1,200 grubbing hoes, 100,000 four-penny nails, 756 fishing hooks, 240 pounds of glass beads, 388 scissors, garden seeds and one set of surgical instruments.*

There is no record of what quantities of beer and brandy survived the trip.

Aboard the *Carolina* were the governor of the expedition, Colonel William Sayle; Captain John West; and an Irish legionnaire Florence O'Sullivan. Sullivan's Island was later named for O'Sullivan despite his reputation as "an ill-natured buggerer of children." Accompanying the officers and ship's crew were ninety-three passengers: twenty-nine men of property and "free persons," sixty-three white indentured servants and one black slave.

The initial settlement was named Albemarle Point, honoring the Duke of Albemarle. The river named Kiawah by the Native Americans was renamed the Ashley River for Lord Anthony Ashley Cooper.

By 1671, boats were arriving from England, Barbados and New York, transporting free men and indentured servants to Carolina. This influx of settlers led to the establishment of two additional settlements: one called Jamestown on a neighboring island, later named James Island, and the other on the point land passed by the *Carolina* on its entry. The settlers called this area Oyster Point or White Point for the oyster shell midden there. The main settlement moved to Oyster Point in April 1672, as it was thought to be the best defensive position for the colony, not necessarily against Native American attack, but against attack by the Spanish now located in St. Augustine. By 1672, the population of the new colony was almost 400: 268 men, 69 women and 59 children.

The island west of the shipping channel delivering the *Carolina* to Albemarle Point is known today as Morris Island. In the eighteenth century, Morris Island was actually three separate, small islands divided by narrow creeks. The northernmost island, Coming's Island or Coming's Point, was named for Captain John Coming. The middle island was known as Morrison's Island and the third island, farthest south, was called Middle Bay Island. Other names for these three islands surfacing on early plats and deeds were Republican Island, Pelican Bank, Mawrice's, Light House Island and Coffin Land.

The first reference to Morris Island in the historic record was August 1670, when Lord Carteret landed the *Carolina* there to cut grass for cattle. Attacked by the Westo Indians, he made a hasty exit.

By 1673, the general assembly authorized the hiring of a man to burn a light every night on Morris Island at the mouth of the harbor, six miles southeast of Oyster Point. These crude "fier balls" were made of tar and pitch, burned in an iron basket sitting on the beach. Every ship entering or leaving the harbor paid a small tax to support the operation of this night beacon. In 1683, French Huguenot Louis Tibon noted that "the port is never without ships and the country is becoming a great traffic center."

By 1700, there were two shipping channels to reach the inner harbor. The main channel, running near Morris Island, was named Pumpkin Hill, thought to be named after an early Morris Island plantation. The second channel was east of Pumpkin Hill, close to Sullivan's Island.

In 1700, the *Rising Sun*, a Scottish gunship, anchored in Charleston Harbor to take on supplies. The ship, carrying 347 passengers, was one of seven vessels transporting passengers returning to Scotland from the failed Darien expedition on the Isthmus of Panama. Aboard ship were Archibald Stobo, a fiery preacher, and his young wife. Hearing of his reputation for passionate sermons, Stobo was invited to preach at the Circular Congregational Church in Charles Town. Stobo, his wife and two others ventured into town for the service and to spend the night while all others remained on the ship.

During the night, Charles Town was besieged by a hurricane. The *Rising Sun* was destroyed, and the next morning all the ship's passengers were drowned and washed ashore on Morris Island. Now stranded in Carolina, Stobo continued to do what he knew best—preach. He continued preaching at Circular Congregational and later founded Presbyterian churches on James Island, John's Island, Wiltown, Cainhoy and Edisto Island.

The "fier" baskets on Morris Island continued to guide ships into the eighteenth century. By 1716, the "light keeper" began using huge tallow candles. Tallow candles, manufactured from animal fat and tissue, became popular in Europe three centuries earlier for street lighting. These large candles required much less maintenance than the "fier" baskets, but did not cast light far enough to sea. These noxious smelling candles gave way to spider lamps burning fish oil, which was, like tallow, a product in plentiful supply.

A guiding light was in high demand in early Charles Town. By the mid-eighteenth century, more than 800 ships a year entered Charles Town Harbor. One inbound visitor reported that "about 350 sail lay off the town."

"A Strange Building"

The advent of the rice culture was creating an economic boom for the Carolinas, and thus, for the Charleston port. Since the early 1700s, Britain required that all Carolina rice be shipped only to Great Britain and its colonies. In September 1730, this restriction was lifted and markets across the world were opened for the prized Carolina Gold rice. From 1730 to 1735, the Charleston port shipped more than forty thousand barrels of rice annually.

Not only was the demand for rice surging, but the price at market rose 67 percent by 1738. This opportunity brought with it a marked increase in acreage under cultivation and a need for slaves to work these growing plantations. The increase in African slaves was so dramatic that a visitor to Charles Town wrote that "Carolina looks more like a Negro Country than like a Country settled by white people." By 1739, Charles Town was the fourth largest city in North America and, perhaps, the wealthiest. The Charles Town port was a busy place.

In 1750, the Commons House of Assembly passed an act to build a permanent lighthouse beacon on Morris Island. However, despite the surging wealth of its residents, the assembly did not have sufficient funds to follow through with its plans. With the act set to expire, the assembly extended the provision for construction to 1765.

In 1757, the funds set aside for the lighthouse were diverted to complete the steeple at Saint Michael's Church. With the ever-increasing port traffic and the urgent need for improved navigational aid through the treacherous harbor channels, King George III ordered a permanent lighthouse to be built. In May 1757, the cornerstone for this first lighthouse was laid on Middle Bay Island. The construction was supervised by architect Samuel Cardy and engineer Thomas Young. Adam Miller, artisan in Charles Town, served as builder and bricklayer, supervising the slaves who built the structure.

One observer commented that the lighthouse was a "strange building, not over fifty feet high and twenty feet in diameter." The lighthouse burned fish oil in lamps suspended from the interior of the lighthouse dome.

Nothing in reports to the assembly reflects the reasons, but the lighthouse was not completed until 1777. The "Charleston Light" was one of the ten pre-Revolutionary lighthouses built in the American colonies.

The harbor operation was critically important to Charles Town. In the eighteenth century, inbound ships delivered new residents, merchants and laborers to fuel the economic machine created by the Lords Proprietors. *Author's Collection.*

This is a copy of a lead plate that was discovered in 1874 when the cornerstone of the 1767 lighthouse was unearthed while digging the foundation of the new lighthouse. *Courtesy of Save the Light.*

Lighthouse	**Date of Construction**
Boston Light on Little Brewster Island	1716
Brant Point Light in Nantucket Harbor	1746
Tybee Island Light, Georgia	1748
Beavertail Light, Narragansett Bay, Rhode Island	1749
New London Light, New London, Connecticut	1760
Sandy Hook Light, New Jersey, New York Harbor	1764
Cape Henlopen Light, Delaware Bay	1767
Charleston Light, Middle Bay Island	1767
Plymouth Light, Massachusetts	1769
Cape Ann, Massachusetts Bay	1771

Once the Revolutionary War began, the colonists extinguished the ten lights so as not to aid the British sea captains attempting to enter these strategic harbors. The Charleston Light was one of only two of these lighthouses to survive the war.

On September 15, 1775, fearing for his safety, Royal Governor William Campbell fled to the HMS *Tamar* anchored in Charleston Harbor. With tensions high, the city's council of safety ordered that Fort Johnson be seized. Colonel William Moultrie led a small force to the James Island fort, finding it unoccupied.

William Henry Drayton, president of the Second Provincial Congress, ordered ships scuttled at the mouth of the Cooper River to prevent access to British ships. The HMS *Tamar* and HMS *Cherokee* opened fire and Drayton had a Patriot ship respond, firing the first shots of the Revolution in Charles Town.

In early 1776, Admiral Sir Peter Parker and General Sir Henry Clinton made plans to capture Sullivan's Island to establish a British outpost and control the ingress and egress through Charleston Harbor. On the morning of June 28, Parker ordered the ships to fire on a hastily constructed Patriot fortification on Sullivan's Island. Clinton was already ashore on Long Island (Isle of Palms) preparing to cross Breach Inlet to flank the Patriot position by land.

The tide and treacherous current through the inlet kept Clinton's force at bay, and the crossing was unsuccessful. The British fleet had twenty ships and 270 guns to focus on Fort Sullivan. The Patriots had only 26 guns and only 28 rounds for each gun. Colonel Moultrie ordered that they fire only once every ten minutes to conserve munitions and discharge only on the closest ship. Though the Americans, trained as infantry and not as artillery, were inexperienced, their fire brought deadly results. Every person on deck of the HMS *Bristol*, the flagship, was killed. Having to man a gun, Royal Governor Campbell received a mortal wound. Admiral Parker had his pants ripped away by wooden splinters aboard ship after an effective blast.

Taking on heavy fire and with three ships run aground on sandbars, the British fleet withdrew to the harbor channel, resulting in the first decisive victory for the Patriots in America. The fleet stayed anchored until mid-July when it set sail for New York.

With the fleet clear, Patriot leader Christopher Gadsden took a force of 120 men to "Light House Island." He sent word to Commander General Charles Lee that they "marched up to the Lighthouse, which was totally deserted, and are now in possession of it."

A 1776 French navigation map of Charleston Harbor noted the location of the lighthouse on Middle Bay Island adjacent to the Pumpkin Hill Channel. The map legend warned of a reef of rocks, stating, "If struck, you will sink immediately."

In February 1780, reports reached Charles Town that a large fleet of British warships were, once again, moving up the coast from the south. In March, British troops, crossing from John's Island, swept across James Island to capture Fort Johnson. The same day, they seized the lighthouse on Middle Bay Island. After a forty-two-day siege, General Lincoln surrendered the last open seaport in America to the British. Charles Town, once the site of America's first decisive victory, was now the home to the Patriot's greatest defeat, with fifty-five hundred men and officers captured. In December 1782, the last of the British troops departed Charles Town, marking the end of the war in the Carolinas.

The South Carolina legislature convened in Charles Town in early 1783 and assumed full governance of the state, including the operation of the lighthouse. In September 1787, the Constitutional Convention in Philadelphia adopted the U.S. Constitution. The "Congress of Confederation" needed a minimum of nine colonies to ratify the constitution before the new government could operate. In June 1788, New Hampshire

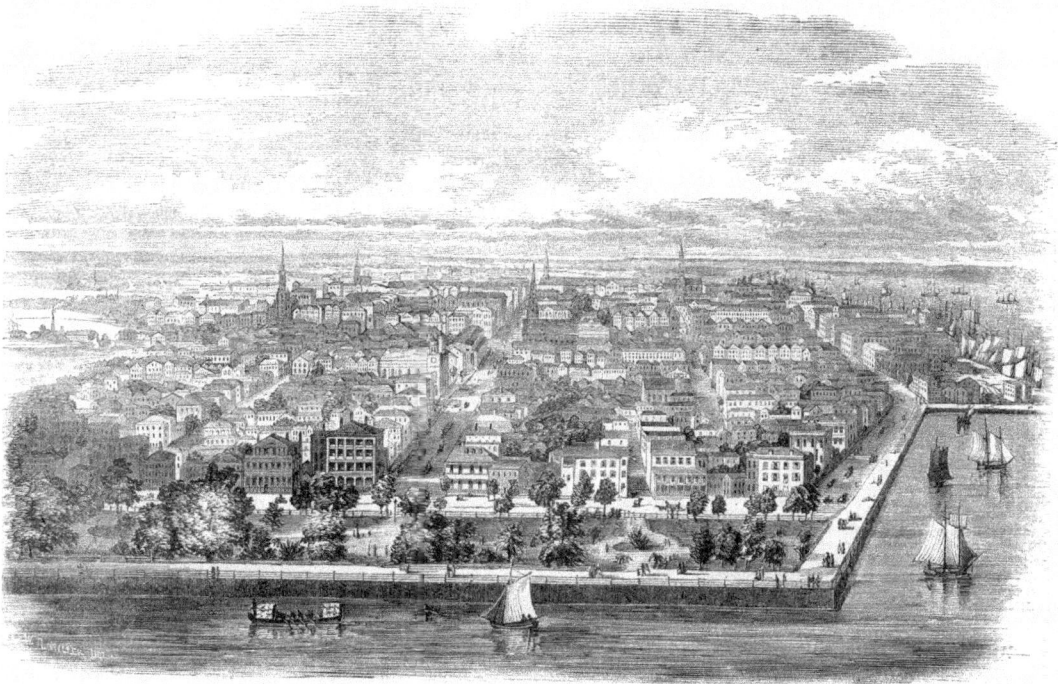

After the Revolutionary War, Charleston was booming with both rice and cotton. Exports in 1816 put the Charleston port second only to New York in value. *Author's Collection.*

became the ninth state to ratify, and in March 1789, the new United States government initiated operations.

On August 7, 1789, Congress passed its ninth law establishing the lighthouse service. This government agency, under the Department of the Treasury, would operate the existing lighthouses in the United States and assume responsibility to build new ones. In 1792, the lighthouse service constructed the Cape Henry Lighthouse in Virginia, guiding ships to the Chesapeake Bay. This lighthouse was the first public works project funded by the new United States government.

On January 20, 1790, the State of South Carolina ceded the

> *lighthouse situated on Middle Bay Island, within the bar of Charleston harbor, bordered to the north by a small inlet called the Folly Inlet, to the east by the Atlantic Ocean, and to the west by a sound or creek.*

The transfer included title to the lighthouse, a modest keeper's house and 565.5 acres of land on Middle Bay Island. In 1790, the only safe entrance to the harbor for deep-draft boats was the Pumpkin Hill Channel, adjacent to Middle Bay Island, at Five Fathom Hole. Following the channel within several hundred yards of Sullivan's Island, the channel turned west to lead to Charleston.

Prior to 1796, President George Washington appointed Daniel Stevens as superintendent for the Charleston lighthouse. Cotton M. Stevens was hired to be the lighthouse keeper at an annual salary of $333.34.

The Second Lighthouse

The date of construction of the second, taller lighthouse is somewhat of a mystery. The first tower was not more than 50 feet in height. Descriptions of the lighthouse in the early nineteenth century tell of a lighthouse 102 feet tall. When the third lighthouse was under construction in the 1870s, workers found the cornerstone for the first one at the same site. Yet, the lighthouse destroyed in 1860 was several miles away.

In 1799, the first lighthouse burned, destroying the woodwork and the lantern. By this date, the main channel had also shifted, and the small creeks separating the three coastal islands had silted in, leaving one large island, now called Morrison's or Morris Island.

In 1801, the lighthouse was rebuilt south of the original location. This new lighthouse was an octagonal brick structure, 102 feet tall from the base to the light. This increased height would allow the light to cast farther out to sea.

The U.S. Lighthouse Service grew rapidly in a country with expansive shorelines and dependant on exports for much of its commerce. From the service's creation in 1790 to 1820, the number of lighthouses increased to 55. By 1852, there were 325 lighthouses and thirty-five lightships serving mariners in the United States.

Appointments as lightkeepers continued to be approved by the president of the United States. In 1806, Albert Gallatin, the secretary of treasury, informed Superintendent Stevens that President Thomas Jefferson had approved the appointment of John Calhoun as "keeper of the Charleston lighthouse."

Many appropriations passed through Congress for the Charleston lighthouse. Repairs were made to the keeper's dwelling, a new kitchen was built and a quarantine station and marine hospital were constructed on the island. In 1808, Congress authorized eighty dollars to buy a horse for the Charleston lightkeeper, but the keeper had "to pay for its maintenance."

In 1811, a United States gunboat struck the reef at Pumpkin Hill Channel and, as foretold in the 1776 French map, the craft quickly sank. The Morris Island keeper helplessly witnessed the accident as the ship and crew all disappeared in the swift channel currents. In a report to Gallatin, he noted that if he was supplied with a boat, he might have saved some of the crew.

In 1812, the Charleston Light was refitted with a revolving light using six reflectors in a lantern, each with a lens in front. This lamp, burning sperm oil, was the new "Winslow Lewis Magnifying and Reflecting Lantern."

The second lighthouse was 102 feet tall, allowing the light to cast farther out to sea. In 1857, the lighthouse was refitted with a first-order Fresnel lens. *Author's Collection.*

Winslow Lewis was a ship's captain in Cape Cod. He developed a new Argand lamp for lighthouse use and received a patent on June 8, 1810. He claimed that the "magnifier" placed in front of each light focused the light beam for greater efficiency. Further, his lantern was cheaper and used 50 percent less oil than the Argand lamps popular in Europe. It was the first of many famous government low bids. Lewis sold his patent to the United States just prior to the War of 1812. All the lighthouses in the country were promptly refitted with the Winslow Lewis lanterns.

The promise of less fuel consumption was true. The new lamps consumed only 24,731 gallons of oil compared to the previous lamps that used more than 52,000 gallons. However, the "magnifiers," green bottle glass placed in front of the flame, accumulated soot quickly, forcing constant cleaning through the night. The lighthouse service later instructed the magnifiers to be removed. Now, compared to the European Argand lamps, the Winslow Lewis lamps were four hundred times less intense.

Lewis also became the main lighthouse contractor in the United States. Some in Congress questioned his construction techniques, calling them substandard, but again, Lewis skillfully was the low bidder.

At public auction in 1825, T.H. Jervey, B.F. Pepoon and A.G. Rose bought the land on Morris Island not owned by the U.S. Lighthouse Service. They planned to develop a town on the northern end of the island. Their plats laid out roadways and 257 lots of .57 acres each. Though nothing reflects the reasoning, the town was never constructed.

The island was popular in the summers as people sought to benefit from the healthy breezes during the "sickly season." One summer visitor in the mid-nineteenth century wrote:

Living so exposed to the ocean there is always plenty of sea breeze which is quite a treat, there are about three or four families living there. We all are near each other and are very intimate, our neighbors being all very sociable and pleasant people.

In March 1835, Congress appropriated $5,000 for five beacons to be built in Charleston to range with the lighthouse. The new lights would coordinate with the main lighthouse, guiding ships through the channel to arrive at the docks on the Cooper River in Charleston. This appropriation was followed by a second appropriation of $6,000 in 1837. The plans were to place one range light on Morris Island, two on Sullivan's Island, one at Castle Pinckney and one final beacon in the city. A major hurricane hit Charleston in September 1854 destroying the keeper's house on Morris Island and the five new beacons and severely damaging the lighthouse.

St. Lo Mellichamp II, the son of his namesake (a lightkeeper in the late 1700s), was the lightkeeper on Morris Island from 1830 to 1856. In 1850, at the age of sixty-five, Mellichamp lived on the island with his second wife, who was twenty-five years his junior, and eight children ranging in ages from twenty-four years to four months old.

Mellichamp was relieved in 1856 by George Wood. Wood operated the lighthouse and assisted with the construction of the new beacons that was underway. By 1855, the beacons on Morris Island, Sullivan's Island and Castle Pinckney were rebuilt. The U.S. Lighthouse Service added a new beacon on Fort Sumter, a new masonry fort that had been under construction since 1829. In 1856, Congress appropriated $2,500 to rebuild the keeper's house. The final beacons were constructed on "the Battery" in Charleston in 1857 and in Mount Pleasant in 1858.

In addition to Wood at the main lighthouse, there were eight other keepers assigned to Charleston. William A. Mellichamp, the son of St. Lo Mellichamp II, was stationed at the south beacon on Morris Island. Gilbert Dudley and James Skillen served as keepers for the beacon at Castle Pinckney. William Read was the keeper for the beacon on the Battery. P.F. Middleton was stationed on Sullivan's Island. Richard Bringloe, William Holmes and James Keanry served as assistant keepers at the main light but would be assigned in the harbor system as needed.

The Lighthouse Service was teeming with controversy about the poorly performing Winslow Lewis lens and the mediocre lighthouses constructed under Lewis contracts. Many in Congress felt that there was collusion between Winslow Lewis and Stephen Pleasonton, the longtime administrator of the U.S. Lighthouse Service.

In 1820, French physicist Augustin-Jean Fresnel developed a new lens specifically for lighthouse applications. This new lens made use of a large aperture and short focal length, allowing the lens to be thinner than a conventional lens but passing light to much longer distances, an obvious advantage for a lighthouse. The first Fresnel lens was installed on the Gironde River in France in 1822. Soon, Scottish physicist Sir David Brewster convinced Great Britain to convert to the Fresnel lens. Shortly thereafter, all of Europe was making use of this new and more effective technology.

Through the 1830s and 1840s, Pleasonton refused to use the Fresnel lens in America. He repeatedly insisted that the operation of the lens was too complicated for the keepers. Finally, in 1851, Congress ordered an investigation of the lighthouse service and the plethora of complaints about the poor quality of America's lighthouses. On October 9, 1852, Congress established a nine-member lighthouse board to oversee and operate the lighthouse service. The board included two Army Corps of Engineers officers, two naval officers, two topographical engineers, two scientists and the secretary of the treasury serving as the board president.

One of the first actions of the new board was to end the thirty-two-year reign of Stephen Pleasonton with his dismissal. They concluded that there was likely no criminal conspiracy between Winslow Lewis and Pleasonton. Lewis was a master promoter of his lens invention and a most effective lobbyist with the lighthouse service and Congress. Pleasonton, an accountant by training, lacked the engineering or maritime background to assess the bids and contracts, instead following the mantra of accepting the low bid.

In 1857, Congress appropriated $15,000 for the installation of a first-order Fresnel lens at the Morris Island lighthouse. The new lenses were available in six sizes or orders. The largest and strongest was the first-order lens, recommended for seacoast lights. The others were intended for range beacons and interior harbor lights.

The first-order lens had more than a thousand individual prisms that were hand ground, hand polished and fitted onto a metal frame. The complete frame for the Morris Island lens was six feet in diameter and twelve feet in height, weighing four tons.

The lens was a work of design art, with a beehive design at the center and concentric rings of glass prisms acting as a magnifying glass to bend the light into a narrow beam.

The Fresnel lens, with more than fifty-thousand candlepower, was 400 percent more effective than the Winslow Lewis Argand lens. The Morris Island Lighthouse first illuminated the new lens on January 1, 1858, casting a light for mariners nineteen miles out to sea. All the Charleston-area beacons were also refitted with small-order Fresnel lenses. The sixth-order lens was installed at the Battery.

By 1860, all lighthouses and beacons in the United States were refitted with new Fresnel lenses.

The "Gate of Hell"

In April 1860, the National Democratic Party Convention, held in Charleston, was a raucous affair over proposals for the party platform guaranteeing the unconditional extension of slavery into the Western territories. After failing to win the platform vote, Southern delegates walked out of the convention, splintering the Democratic Party.

The Southern Democrats nominated John C. Breckinridge. The Northern Democrats reconvened in Baltimore and nominated Stephen A. Douglas. Knowing this split ticket virtually ensured the election of Republican Abraham Lincoln, Southern governors began discussing secession. South Carolinians had a well-earned reputation as being arrogant political hotheads. William Henry Trescott, a South Carolinian and former assistant secretary of state in the Buchanan administration, suggested that Georgia must lead the secession movement to secure the full support of the other Southern states. He wrote: "Give her [Georgia] all the glory…We must cut up by the roots some home ambitions and much home selfishness." Others suggested that Alabama lead the effort, a proposal to which South Carolina Congressman Lawrence Keitt responded, "If we wait for Alabama, we will wait eternally."

As expected, Lincoln was elected by a large margin, but the news still shocked Charleston when it reached the city on November 7, 1860. Secession fever was rampant. Within days, all of South Carolina's congressional delegation resigned their positions. On November 10, impatient at Georgia's hesitation, the South Carolina General Assembly enacted a bill calling for a secession convention.

The secession convention opened in Columbia on December 17. Fears about a smallpox outbreak caused the convention to move to Charleston the next day. As the convention reconvened, the lighthouse superintendent sent a telegram to Washington stating that he expected the South Carolina troops to seize the Morris Island Lighthouse.

On December 20, Commander Semmes, secretary of the lighthouse board, wrote Secretary of the Treasury Philip Thomas that he would not recommend that the service illuminate the coast of South Carolina against the will of the state government. That same evening, the secession convention, by unanimous vote, seceded from the United States, creating the Republic of South Carolina.

The Charleston lighthouse superintendent again sent a telegram to Semmes, writing:

The Governor of the State of South Carolina has requested me to leave the state. I am informed that forcible possession has been taken of the [Morris Island] lighthouse, buoys and beacons of the harbor and that similar measures will be adapted to all lights in the State.

The lighthouse was still staffed by George Wood, who arrived in 1856. George lived on the island with his wife Hannah; his son William, who served as assistant keeper; William's two children, John and Mary; and assistant keeper William Lowridge. Once the lighthouse was seized, they left Morris Island.

The Rattlesnake Shoal lightship was seized and towed into Charleston Harbor and the remaining lighthouse tenders were seized. The light at Morris Island and all the supporting beacons were extinguished.

Even though South Carolina had seceded, the United States government still had a military presence at the government arsenal in town: Castle Pinckney in the harbor; Fort Johnson on James Island; Fort Sumter, which was still under construction; and at Fort Moultrie, a garrison of sixty-one men, seven officers and a regimental band of thirteen musicians. The Federal troops in Charleston were commanded by Major Robert Anderson, who had only arrived a month earlier.

After Christmas, Anderson moved his troops, under the cover of darkness, to Fort Sumter, a more defensible position. When authorities in Charleston learned of Anderson's move, the state troops quickly seized Fort Johnson, Castle Pinckney and Fort Moultrie. On December 30, Governor Pickens ordered the seizure of the U.S. arsenal in Charleston.

The next day, Pickens ordered that a battery be erected on Morris Island to command the entrance to the shipping channel into Charleston Harbor. This site, named Fort Morris, was manned by forty cadets from the Citadel, flying a red palmetto flag and armed with four twenty-four-pound field howitzers, guns that could reach any ship entering the channel. The state authorities removed the Fresnel lens from the lighthouse and stationed cadets there as well to act as lookouts.

On January 7, 1861, news reached Charleston that the steamship *Star of the West*, commanded by Captain McGown, was bound for Charleston with armed reinforcements and supplies for Anderson and the garrison at Fort Sumter. On the morning of January 9, the *Star of the West* entered the channel of the harbor. The cadets, commanded by Major Peter Stevens, fired a warning shot across the bow of the Union steamship. When the steamer did not yield, the cadets opened fire on the vessel, hitting the bow, rudder and the ship's rigging. Knowing he would soon come into range of the other South Carolina batteries, McGown turned his ship and left the channel without reinforcing and resupplying Anderson. Thus, the actual first shot of the War Between the States was fired by cadets stationed on Morris Island.

On January 31, the attorney general for the Republic of South Carolina wrote to Washington, offering to purchase Fort Sumter and the other Federal fortifications in Charleston. The offer was refused.

Episcopal priest Reverend Toomer Porter, in his reminiscences of the war, wrote of a conversation in early 1861 he had on the Battery with Colonel James Chesnut,

This woodcut engraving that appeared in *Harper's Weekly* depicts the Citadel cadets at the hastily constructed Fort Morris firing on the *Star of the West*, attempting to resupply Major Anderson and the garrison at Fort Sumter. *Author's Collection.*

former U.S. senator from South Carolina. Toomer remarked, "These are troubled times, Colonel; we are at the beginning of a terrible war." Chesnut naïvely responded, "There will be no war, it will be arraigned. I will drink all the blood shed in the war."

In February 1861, Jefferson Davis, president of the newly formed Confederate States of America, appointed Pierre Gustave Toutant Beauregard to the rank of brigadier general and dispatched him to Charleston to assume command of the Confederate forces. Ironically, Beauregard and Anderson were well acquainted. While at West Point, Beauregard's favorite instructor was Professor of Artillery Robert Anderson. After graduation, Beauregard remained at West Point as Anderson's assistant.

Beauregard immediately reinforced batteries on Fort Johnson and Sullivan's Island, while constructing new batteries on Morris Island. The stage was set. Anderson and his small garrison were defiantly burrowed in at Fort Sumter. The amassed guns of Charleston were trained on him and tensions were high.

Finally, on April 11, Beauregard sent a message to his mentor Anderson proposing:

All proper facilities will be afforded for the removal of yourself and your command, together with company arms and property, and all private property, to any post in the United States which you may select.

Anderson responded to his former student simply: "It is a demand with which I regret that my sense of honor, and obligations to my government, prevent my compliance."

The next morning a mortar shot was fired from Fort Johnson to Fort Sumter signaling the beginning of a relentless barrage of hot shot and shell on the Union garrison. After more than thirty-two hours of constant attack, with his fort in flames and his own munitions exhausted, Anderson ordered the garrison flag to be lowered, replacing it with a white bedsheet to indicate surrender. Celebrations erupted through the South, alarms sounded in the North, but neither side could appreciate what this first engagement would mean for the coming years.

By late April 1861, more than 164 lighthouses and beacons from Virginia to Texas were darkened. The only lights allowed to burn were those in the Florida reefs, where even local captains would not risk travel without proper guidance.

Even though Anderson's small garrison had been driven out of Charleston, state authorities anticipated that the Union army and navy would return to take the city with a vengeance. Understanding the strategic importance of Charleston and Savannah, President Davis sent Robert E. Lee to oversee the preparation of the coastal defenses. The same day that Lee arrived in Charleston by train, a great Union fleet of seventy-seven ships and twelve thousand troops attacked and captured Fort Beauregard on Eddings Island, South Carolina, and Fort Walker on Hilton Head. The Union forces set up their Department of the South at Port Royal, South Carolina, and Charleston prepared for attack.

After Confederate General Beauregard failed to obtain Anderson's agreement to evacuate Fort Sumter, he ordered the attack for April 12, 1861. Before dawn, a mortar at Fort Johnson on James Island fired a shot over Fort Sumter to signal the bombardment. *Author's Collection.*

The citizens of Charleston watched the bombardment from the Battery and the rooftops of homes with a harbor view. Though this *Harper's Weekly* engraving depicts the women crying and visibly upset, in truth, great celebrations erupted all through the port city over the much-anticipated start to the war. *Author's Collection.*

The Confederates developed a well-prepared system of defense for Charleston, including harbor obstructions, well-protected batteries to repulse a naval attack and defensive lines on James Island to receive a land attack. They correctly believed that a Union attack would focus on Morris Island, where Union batteries could then shell not only the harbor defenses, but also the city itself. Charleston, after all, was not only the site of the first hostilities, but also was the main blockade-running port, keeping the Confederacy supplied.

Preparing for the inevitable assault, Confederate command decided to destroy the lighthouse to prevent its use as a lookout tower for Union reconnaissance. An article in the December 20, 1861 edition of the Charleston *Mercury* noted:

> *The report reached us yesterday morning that the Charleston lighthouse, situated on Morris Island, and which for many years has guided the mariner to our harbor, was blown up on Wednesday night, by order of the military authorities. Nothing save a heap of ruins now marks the spot where it stood.*

There were conflicting stories about what happened to the valuable first-order Fresnel lens removed in early 1861. Many believe that the lens was also destroyed by the Confederates. A competing legend is that the lens was buried by the Confederates and, after the war, was sent to California for the new Pigeon Point Lighthouse, south of San Francisco.

In April 1863, Union Admiral Samuel Du Pont arrived at Charleston Harbor with his fleet of ironclad ships. As the "invincible" fleet attacked, it was met with the combined force of seventy-six guns at Fort Sumter, Batteries Bee and Beauregard with Fort Moultrie on Sullivan's Island, and Batteries Wagner and Gregg on Morris Island. Several ironclads were damaged and the USS *Keokuk* was lost. An embarrassed Du Pont withdrew to Port Royal.

On June 12, 1863, General Quincy A. Gillmore was given command of the Department of the South and Admiral John A. Dahlgren assumed command of the Union fleet from the defeated Du Pont. Gillmore moved his troops from Port Royal to Folly Island and soon crossed the inlet to establish a stronghold on the southern end of Morris Island. Knowing the terrain from experience, Du Pont wrote to his wife, "I pity the poor soldiers if they land there."

The Union troops built a lookout tower atop the lighthouse rubble and established housing in the old smallpox hospital and quarantine station. The small sand island was to be the stage for one of the greatest confrontations of the war. The 1,620 men at Battery Wagner would face a Union army of 11,000 men and a heavily armed fleet.

Gillmore and Dahlgren decided on a bold frontal attack on Battery Wagner, the Confederate stronghold on Morris Island. At midday on July 18, 1863, the Union fleet and land batteries on southern Morris Island initiated an intense bombardment of Battery Wagner. After eleven hours of steady bombardment, Gillmore ordered his infantry attack. Union Colonel Haldimand S. Putnam was commanding one of the lead Union brigades. He remarked that they were heading to Wagner "like a flock of sheep." Putnam died in the attack after being shot in the head.

General Gillmore set his base of operations on Morris Island for the siege on Battery Wagner. This photograph is of Gillmore standing in front of his headquarters tent. *Courtesy of the Library of Congress.*

The Union army first captured the south end of Morris Island. General Gillmore created a lookout tower built atop the ruins of the lighthouse. *Courtesy of the Library of Congress.*

The ill-fated attack was devastating for the Union infantry advancing on the sand fort. The Fifty-fourth Massachusetts, the first black regiment mustered for the Union army, led the attack and received the brunt of the determined defense. Its commander Colonel Robert Shaw and more than half the regiment would be killed. During the attack, Sergeant William Carney of the Fifty-fourth seized the fallen Union flag and, even after being wounded, bravely carried the standard in the attack. He later became the first African American ever awarded the Congressional Medal of Honor.

A Connecticut lieutenant observed:

> *I had been in several battles before in Virginia…but nothing in my experience compared with the slaughter in front and in Fort Wagner that night…The dead and wounded covered it* [the seaward wall] *so that it was impossible to get around. All of our commanding officers were either killed or wounded.*

Once the attack ended late that night, the Union casualties were 1,515 compared to 174 for the Confederates. An officer with the Forty-eighth New York remarked that Wagner was "the gate of Hell."

After the failed assault, both armies settled in for a long siege. The Confederates placed large numbers of torpedoes and mines on the beachfront combined with a system of rifle pits in front of Battery Wagner. The Union engineers countered this by digging a series of zigzag trenches to meticulously advance on the Confederate position.

The Morris Island siege lasted fifty-eight days before the thousand Confederates stealthily evacuated Batteries Wagner and Gregg on Morris Island to prevent their capture. The Union army learned of the evacuation by deserters crossing the Union

This engraving, printed in *Harper's Weekly*, depicts the charge of the Fifty-fourth Massachusetts on Battery Wagner. Their commander, Colonel Robert Shaw, challenged his men, "Take the fort or die there." More than half of the regiment did die during the failed attack. *Author's Collection.*

lines early in the morning of September 7. Gillmore signaled to Dahlgren aboard ship, stating, "The whole island is ours, but the enemy has escaped us."

One North Carolina soldier, stationed at Battery Wagner, would write of his experience:

> *I have heard preachers talk about Hell, a great big hole, full of fire and brimstone, where a bad fellow was dropped in, and I will allow it used to worry me at times, but Gentlemen, Hell can't be worse than Battery Wagner. I have got out of that, and the other place ain't going to worry me any more!*

Early in the siege, Clara Barton, the future founder of the Red Cross, established a hospital on the south end of Morris Island, about a mile north of the lighthouse site. She later wrote:

> *We have captured one fort—Gregg—and one charnel house—Wagner—and we have built one cemetery, Morris Island. The thousand little sand hills that in the pale moonlight are a thousand headstones, and the restless ocean waves that roll and breakup on the whitened beach sing an eternal requiem to the toll-worn gallant dead who sleep beside.*

The Union army set up operations in the former Confederate batteries, renaming them Fort Putnam and Fort Strong for two of the Union officers killed in the grand

The photograph is of the beacon house on Morris Island after the attack on Battery Wagner, July 18, 1863. The skeletal remains of the house was the headquarters for General W.H. Davis of the 104th Pennsylvania and served as a signal station for Gillmore. *Courtesy of the U.S. Coast Guard.*

Temporary barracks had to be constructed for the eleven thousand Union troops assembled on Morris Island. Supplying, housing and feeding this large army in the field was an enormous logistical challenge. In the background, one of the keepers' dwellings was converted for use by the army. *Courtesy of the Library of Congress.*

This birds-eye view engraving of Charleston Harbor, published in *Harper's Weekly*, provided an excellent understanding of the location of Union and Confederate forces in 1863 during the siege on Battery Wagner. *Author's Collection.*

Key:

1–Charleston & Savannah Railroad
2–Ashley River
3–Charleston
4–Cooper River
5–Wando River
6–Castle Pinckney
7–Fort Ripley

8–Fort Johnson (James Island)
9–Stono River
10–Fort Sumter
11–Fort Moultrie
12–Battery Gregg (Morris Is.)
13–Fort Wagner

14–Union Advanced batteries
15–Captured works on Morris Is.
16–Lighthouse Inlet
17–Union Battery- Folly Island
18–Union fleet
19–Hotel

20–Sullivan's Island
21–Moultrieville
22–Mount Pleasant
23–Breach Inlet
24–Shem Creek
0,0–Confederate batteries (James Island)

assault on Battery Wagner. The siege on Charleston would continue until the Confederate army evacuated Charleston in February 1865. The entire region was devastated by the nineteen-month siege, the longest of the war. General William T. Sherman, when visiting Charleston in May, observed:

> *Anyone who is not satisfied with war should go and see Charleston, and he will pray louder and deeper than ever that the country may in the long future be spared any more war.*

As soon as Federal forces occupied Charleston, the shipping channel was illuminated with temporary beacons. By 1866, most of the lighthouses still standing in the South were restored to service.

"Engaged on Public Works"

Peter Conover Hains, the son of a poor Philadelphia shoemaker, was a most unlikely person to ensure the return of Charleston's seacoast light. Hains entered the U.S. Military Academy at West Point in 1857. His class graduated in June 1861 and rushed into service on both sides of the war. The Class of '61 produced thirty-one Union officers, twenty-one Confederate officers and nine generals. More than half of the class was killed in action during America's greatest conflict.

Hains's classmates included the infamous General George Armstrong Custer; Adelbert Ames, the Reconstruction governor of Mississippi; Thomas Lafayette Rosser, Confederate general, railroad engineer for the Dakota and Montana territories and surveyor of the Yellowstone region; John Whitney Barlow, Union general and engineer who was famous for his *Report of a Reconnaissance of the Basin of the Upper Yellowstone in 1871*; Henry Algernon du Pont, largest stockholder of the family chemical company, U.S. senator and author; Judson Kilpatrick, U.S. diplomat to Chile and playwright; Orville E. Babcock, private secretary to President Ulysses S. Grant; Pierce M.B. Young, Confederate general, U.S. congressman and U.S. diplomat to Russia, Guatemala and Honduras; John J. Garnett, Confederate colonel, poet and author of works on Robert E. Lee and Ulysses S. Grant; and Emory Upton, noted as the "class genius," author and renowned expert on military training and tactics.

President Lincoln attended the class graduation on June 24, 1861, commenting to Secretary of War Stanton, "A fine crop, a fine crop Mr. Secretary!"

Upon graduation, Hains was assigned to the Second U.S. Artillery. He noted later in his writings:

> *I was assigned to train a gun-crew over at what is now Fort Meyer, Virginia, just across the river from Washington. It was a great gun—a thirty-pounder Parrott rifle, drawn by ten horses as green as could be, horses from the farm that had not been trained to pull together…some 200 men were attached to the gun…The piece weighed 6,000 pounds.*

Hains and the Second Artillery were part of the Federal troops amassed for the upcoming battle at Bull Run, Virginia. Hains wrote of his experiences in 1911 for *Cosmopolitan* magazine in an article entitled "The First Gun at Bull Run."

This photograph, taken at Fair Oaks, Virginia, prior to the Battle of Bull Run, was of the brigade officers of the Horse Artillery commanded by Lieutenant Colonel William Hay. Lieutenant Hains is in the middle row, second from the left. *Courtesy of the Library of Congress.*

Three shots at daylight will be the signal for the fight to begin...and as my giant gun was the loudest speaker of the whole armies it was chosen...I would open the fight between the armies of the North and the South.

At a little after six o'clock on as peaceful-appearing a Sabbath morning as that countryside ever knew, the order came. I sighted the rifle carefully, and the men grinned their delight. Then I stood back. "Fire!"...I followed that shot with two others, and the signal had been given to McDowell's army that they were to begin hostilities. The first big battle of the Civil War had begun.

Hains was later assigned to Grant's army for the Vicksburg campaign in 1863. He was an engineer in the Thirteenth Corps in the Union Army of Tennessee. After his superior became ill, Hains was thrust into the limelight as Grant's chief engineer. A noted journal, the *Military Engineer*, published Hains's article "The Vicksburg Campaign" in 1921. Hains wrote of the great siege:

Grant was no stickler for the rules either of strategy or logistics as laid down in the books...He followed the dictates of common sense. One fundamental rule, is that is wise to do that which your antagonist does not think you will do, and to avoid what he thinks you will do.

The siege [Vicksburg] *lasted just 42 days, only two over the number laid down in our books as allowable.*

The magnitude of Grant's victory was amazing, even to ourselves. He totally destroyed an army almost as large as his own, captured guns of all calibers, besides about 6,000 muskets, caused the surrender of Port Hudson with all its armament and about 6,000 more men, opened the Mississippi to the navigation of the great northwest, broke the Confederacy into two pieces, destroyed almost absolutely all communication of the Confederacy with foreign nations, cut in two the lines of supply the Confederacy had established to Mexico, and carried dismay to the hearts of the southern people, many of whom saw the fall of Vicksburg the downfall of the Southern Confederacy.

Grant said of his chief engineer, "Captain Hains is a most excellent officer and was by me recommended for the Colonelcy of a New Jersey regiment more than a year since."

Even during the war, Hains found time for a courtship, marrying Virginia Pettis Jenkins, the daughter of Rear Admiral Thornton A. Jenkins.

At the end of the war, Hains accepted a position as engineer with the U.S. Lighthouse Service. He was quickly appointed as district engineer for the sixth lighthouse district on the southeast coast. In this position, he oversaw the construction of the new lighthouses on Morris Island and St. Augustine.

In 1874, Hains accepted the position of secretary of the lighthouse board in Washington, D.C. While serving as secretary he translated Leonce Reynaud's *Memoir Upon the Illumination and Beaconage of the Coasts of France*.

Leaving the U.S. Lighthouse Service in 1879, Hains transferred to the Army Corps of Engineers. His first assignment was the design of river improvements for the Potomac, James and Shenandoah Rivers. In Washington, he solved a longstanding problem with a foul-smelling swamp of 650 acres at the Potomac Flats with the creation of the Tidal Basin. A beautiful park filled with the famous Japanese cherry trees was named Hains Point in his honor.

His distinguished career continued with significant service on both the Nicaragua Canal and Panama Canal commissions. Hains was the engineer to successfully mount an argument to build the canal in Panama.

Hains was promoted to lieutenant colonel in 1886 and colonel in 1895. During the Spanish-American War in 1898, he served as brigadier general of volunteers and commander of the Third Division of the First Corps. He was involved in the capture of Guyama and Las Palmas, Puerto Rico.

After the war, Hains built the National Road from Aqueduct Bridge to Mount Vernon, today known as the George Washington Parkway.

He became a prolific writer for magazines and military journals. While serving with the Panama Commission, Hains wrote a fascinating article predicting:

Japan, a young and vigorous naval power, occupies a favorable geographic position to operate against us in the far east…An attack on the Philippines is within the limits of probability. If successful, Japan might make a naval demonstration as far eastward as our Pacific coast…An

Hains was the chief engineer for General Grant during the siege of Vicksburg. Hains's design promoted one of the most decisive victories for the Union army in the Mississippi region. This monument is placed on the Vicksburg National Park site in Hains's honor. *Courtesy of Save the Light.*

General Peter Conover Hains, the engineer who supervised the construction of the Morris Island Lighthouse, was the only American officer to serve in the Civil War, the Spanish-American War and World War I. *Courtesy of Colonel Peter C. Hains.*

This photograph is of Peter C. Hains, retired brigadier general, walking with his son, P.C. Hains II in New York. *Courtesy of the Library of Congress.*

adequate defense of a fortified Isthmian canal can be made in no other way than by providing a navy of sufficient power to control the seas at either terminus.

U.S. Senator Mark Hanna asked of Hains in 1902, "What line of work have you done?" Hains modestly responded in a grand understatement, "Well, I have been engaged on public works of various kinds ever since 1863."

Hains retired in 1904 as a brigadier general in the regular army. He continued his career writing until the outbreak of World War I. By direction of the president of the United States and an act of Congress on September 18, 1917, Hains was placed on active duty as a major general. General Hains was engineer for the Norfolk Harbor and River District and in command of defensive works at Hampton Roads, Virginia. He was the only American officer to serve in the Civil War, the Spanish-American War and World War I.

Hains retired for the second time in September 1918. He died at Walter Reed Army Hospital on November 7, 1921, and was buried with military honors at Arlington National Cemetery. *Military Engineer* magazine wrote of Hains, "In depth of devotion to his work…and in the range of activities, his record has seldom been equaled."

An unusual family, Hains's sons graduated from West Point and Annapolis. His grandson, General P.C. Hains III, graduated West Point in 1924 and was a highly decorated hero in World War II. His sons and grandson are also buried in Arlington. His great-grandson, P.C. Hains IV, and great-great-grandson, John Tower Hains, both graduated West Point and served their country with distinguished careers in the army.

Shining Once Again

After the war, Morris Island was a godforsaken place. One Union soldier who served on the island recalled:

> *I have visited all parts of the island, the regiments, the batteries, the forts, the hospitals, the depots, the ruins of the lighthouse, the skeleton of the keeper's house, the old batteries that triumphed over rebel strongholds, the vicinity of the "Swamp Angel," the solemn graveyards... Henceforth this island is peculiarly the property of the muse of history.*

Another soldier spoke of the bleak conditions:

> *This Morris Island is the most desolate heap of sand-hills I ever saw. It is so barren that you cannot find so much as a gypsum weed growing...The beach at some points is at least 1/3 of a mile in width.*

R.H. Cornwell, a Boston reporter, visited the island to chronicle the site after the fall of Charleston. He met a veteran of the Fifty-fourth Massachusetts living, with his family, in an old bombproof shelter at Battery Gregg. The former soldier was harvesting iron and scrap metal abandoned by both armies all over the island and selling it by the ton.

Cornwell also wrote of the many hundreds of buried soldiers as they were exposed by the eroding shoreline. He reflected:

> *A sad sight met our eyes when, following our guide, we reached the level sea beach. Human skeletons from the sea had washed the sand lay grinning upon the shoreline and fill us with sad sensations which still haunt our dreams.*

The U.S. government offered a bounty to gravediggers willing to excavate bodies of fallen soldiers for reinterment at the Beaufort National Cemetery. The bounty was paid for each skeleton delivered.

The gravediggers complained vehemently that in most cases the bodies were originally interred in mass graves and that, in quick order, the remains became quickly mixed up with others. In response, the bounty regulation was amended to pay on each skull delivered. The gravediggers quickly complied, but only delivered the skulls, making no effort to excavate the full skeletons. The unintended consequence was the mass of human bones left on sites like Morris Island. In 1866, these exposed remains created such an unhealthy situation that even the quarantine station was moved from Morris Island to Fort Johnson on James Island.

Surveys of the Charleston Harbor channels revealed that the deep channels had again shifted. There were now two channels available to deep-draft ships: the Pumpkin Hill Channel and a South Channel. With the lighthouse destroyed, Congress moved quickly to establish range lights on Morris Island, appropriating $15,000 in March 1867.

A hastily constructed temporary beacon was established on the ruins at Fort Sumter by 1866 until a more permanent structure could be completed. Like Fort Sumter, a thirty-five-foot skeleton frame beacon was constructed on Morris Island south of the intended lighthouse site. The lighthouse tender *Maggie* was also assigned to the Charleston channel to augment the beacons. The Battery beacon was reinstalled with a sixth-order Fresnel lens as the terminus for the shipping channel.

The U.S. Lighthouse Service approved the hiring of one keeper to maintain the two beacons on Morris Island. Mr. C.K. Smith was hired at the rate of $100 per month and subsistence of $1 per day while in the field.

This temporary beacon was hastily built atop the ruins at Fort Sumter. It was later replaced by a more permanent structure. *Courtesy of the Library of Congress.*

The Morris Island Lighthouse and the coastal beacons were augmented by lighthouse tenders that could be easily moved where and when needed. Note the beacon lights on top of each mast. This tender is Lightship #34, stationed in Charleston. *Author's Collection.*

Once Fort Sumter was restored, a suitable range light was built at the fort. The beacon was equipped with a sixth-order Fresnel lens. Note the beacon on the left center of the fort. *Courtesy of the U.S. Coast Guard.*

By the early 1870s, more permanent beacons were erected at the key harbor locations. Two beacons were constructed on Morris Island in 1870 and 1872, each equipped with a fifth-order Fresnel lens. Between 1872 and 1876, beacons were constructed on Sullivan's Island. One beacon with a sixth-order lens was first located at Fort Moultrie, and later, by 1879, was reestablished outside the fort. The second light, a rear beacon, had a fourth-order Fresnel light.

The beacon at Castle Pinckney was rebuilt with a fifth-order Fresnel lens. By 1869, the Battery beacon was replaced with a beacon in the steeple of Saint Philip's Church to relocate the beacon directly on line with the shipping channel.

With beacons and a lightship in place, attention was turned to the main lighthouse intended for Morris Island. On March 3, 1873, Congress appropriated $60,000 for "commencing the rebuilding of a first order seacoast light on Morris Island destroyed during the war." This first appropriation allowed the engineering assessments to begin. Major Peter C. Hains was the engineer for the South Carolina lighthouse district. He picked the logical site for the lighthouse to be constructed based on soil conditions and the relationship to the current shipping channel.

As initial excavation was taking place, workers discovered the cornerstone for the first Morris Island lighthouse in 1767. They recovered a lead plate that had an etching of the first lighthouse and a plate honoring those participating in the project.

The photograph is the front beacon constructed on Morris Island. This range light was established in 1870. Note the shades drawn in the lantern room during daylight. Direct sunlight hitting the lens during the day could create enough heat to cause the lantern room to combust. *Courtesy of the National Archives.*

The south range light on Morris Island, shown in this photograph, was constructed in 1870. *Courtesy of the National Archives.*

An assistant keepers' dwelling located on Morris Island outside of the main lighthouse complex was constructed after the Civil War. The keepers housed here were responsible for the range lights on the island, designed to compliment the lighthouse. *Courtesy of the National Archives.*

This interesting beacon was built on Sullivan's Island in 1879. It was equipped with a sixth-order Fresnel lens. Note Fort Moultrie just behind the beacon and the rear range light in the far background on the right. *Courtesy of the U.S. Coast Guard.*

The historic Saint Philip's Church steeple was the last beacon for the system of Charleston Harbor lights. The church was on line with the terminus of the shipping channel. This light replaced the beacon at the Battery. *Author's Collection.*

Hains reported:

The soil is very soft to a comfortable depth, utterly wanting in bearing capacity for such a structure as a lighthouse tower, and the cheapest way to overcome this difficulty will be to drive piles.

His first report to Professor Joseph Henry, chairman of the U.S. Lighthouse Board, dated December 18, 1873, noted the results of his soil borings:

0–2 feet	fine, light-colored sand mixed with loam
2–4 feet	fine sand, darker color and more free of loam
4–5 feet	sand, still darker
5–7 feet	sand and mud mixture
7–9 feet	sticking mud without sand
9–13 feet	mud and sand
13–14 feet	sand, mud and shell
14–17 feet	mud and shell
17–57 feet	soft mud

Hains drove a test pile made of yellow pine, twelve inches in diameter, nineteen feet long and sharpened on the point. The pile was set in a hole three feet deep and sank six more inches on its own weight. Using an engineering calculation known as the "Sanders formula," the test pile could bear 7.5 tons.

He estimated the weight of the proposed lighthouse tower to be four thousand tons, creating a need for 210 piles for the foundation, each bearing a load of nineteen tons. His recommendation to the lighthouse board was to use piles fifteen inches in diameter, set in rows two feet and ten inches measured center to center. With this formation each pile could bear as much as twenty tons, giving "security of settlement without help from the grillage and concrete."

Enhancing the load-bearing capacity as much as possible, Hains recommended the piles be sawed off seven feet below the ground surface and capped with two sets of twelve- by twelve-inch pieces "tree-nailed" to the head of each pile. These would be notched and "tree-nailed" to each other. This would form a grillage eighteen inches in thickness. The space in between the piles to a depth of three feet would be filled with concrete. On top of the concrete, a foundation of masonry rubble would be built.

Work on driving the piles commenced in the fall of 1873. The lighthouse board also approved the contract for the needed ironwork. With work now underway, Hains reported to the lighthouse board again in March 1874. He revised his weight calculations, writing, "A more careful estimate places the weight [of the tower] at 3,200 tons." Strengthening the foundation, Hains also increased the size of the base to twenty-two feet and was driving piles at two-feet, eight-inch centers rather than the planned two-feet, ten-inch centers. This change increased the total number of piles to 264 and distributed only twelve tons of weight to each pile, which had a capacity of twenty tons.

In a final measure intended to strengthen the foundation, Hains reported that he intended to leave the cofferdam needed for construction in place once completed. He would cut the sheet piling off at the waterline and fill the dam and piles with concrete to twenty feet. He noted, "By using Portland cement and making the mortar rich, the mass can be made as strong as a single rock."

In December 1873, Hains received a telegram from Professor Henry in Washington requesting that work on the Morris Island lighthouse cease. Henry indicated that the board was reconsidering the project. Hains quickly responded that his project was well underway. The temporary quarters for the workers were already constructed; the storehouse was built; the wharf for landing building materials was in place; the contract for the ironwork had already been awarded; and the "illuminating apparatus" had already been purchased. Hains continued by defending the importance of the project, stating:

> *I would also call your attention to the importance of this lighthouse. Charleston is rapidly becoming one of the most important ports of entry for large ships engaged in the cotton trade. There is no seacoast light between Cape Romain and Tybee Island, a distance of about 100 miles.*

Satisfied with both the progress on construction and Hains's defense of the need for the lighthouse, the board relented and approved Hains to continue construction.

By June 1874, 70 of the required 264 piles were installed. The work was suspended for the summer to avoid the Lowcountry "sickly season." The same month, Congress approved the second appropriation of $60,000 for the Morris Island project.

By November 1874, all 264 piles were installed. As required, they were cut off and capped to form the grillage design. The base of the tower was eight feet thick below ground and thirty-six feet in diameter at the surface. In March 1875, Congress passed the final appropriation of $30,000 to complete the project.

Once complete, the tower was thirty-three feet in diameter at the base and sixteen feet, eight inches at the top. The lighthouse tower was constructed with two shells of brickwork. Hains reported:

> *The inner one being cylindrical and connected to the outer one with six radial walls. The inner and outer walls decrease in thickness as they approach the top.*

The thickness of the outer wall was 3 feet, 9 inches at the base and narrowing to 1 foot, 10 ½ inches at the top, using more than a million bricks. The distance from the ground to the focal plane of the lantern was 150 feet, with a total height of 158 feet.

Beginning in the 1850s, the U.S. Lighthouse Board prescribed color schemes for the lighthouse towers to assist mariners with their identification in daylight. The Morris Island Lighthouse was painted in alternating bands of black and white.

Inside the tower, an iron stairway of nine flights led to the lantern room. This "floating" stairway is not connected to the walls, but only attached at the bottom and

The Morris Island Lighthouse was first illuminated on October 1, 1876. On the left is the keepers' dwelling housing the families of the head keeper and his two assistants. *Courtesy of Jim Booth.*

The Fresnel Lens

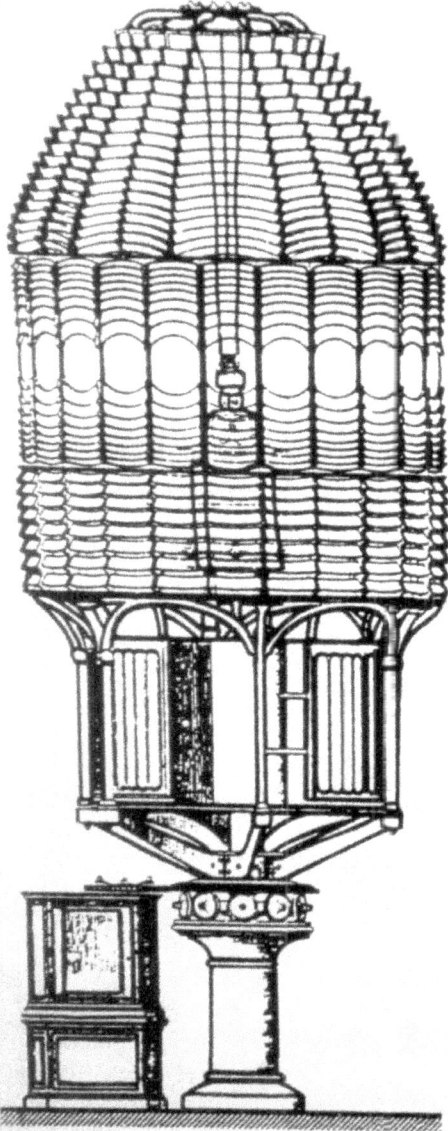

Hunting Island Lighthouse was deactivated in 1933, and the disposition of its second-order Fresnel lens is unknown.

This partial lens is similar to the Hunting Island lens and was originally housed in the Morris Island Lighthouse in Charleston. It was transferred here for exhibit in the early 1960s when the Morris light was replaced.

Invented by French physicist Augustin Fresnel, this lens became the standard for American lighthouses in the 1850s. Its precision ground glass prisms concentrated the light from oil-fueled lamps into a beam which projected great distances.

These lens were classified by size into seven categories or "orders." The first-order lens was the largest and used in the most critically located light stations.

The Hunting Island lens was a smaller second-order Fresnel lens which cast a beam of 100,000 candlepower that could be seen from 18 miles at sea.

As a seacoast light, a first-order Fresnel lens was installed at the Morris Island Lighthouse. The lens was twelve feet tall and six feet in diameter, weighing 12,800 pounds. The lens was made of more than a thousand individual prisms, which had to be cleaned and polished every day. *Courtesy of Save the Light.*

the top. The design allows for its own support and stability. On the east and west faces of the tower are "segmented-arched head windows."

The lantern was outfitted with a first-order Fresnel lens, the latest technology and the proper-sized light for a seacoast lighthouse. The lens had more than a thousand individual prisms and weighed more than 12,800 pounds. These Fresnel lenses were a major investment, as a first-order lens in 1873 cost $10,000. The lens for Morris Island was fixed white with an arc of 270 degrees. It had a visibility of nineteen miles out to sea.

The lantern room originally had glass storm panes. The top of the room had a stormproof ventilator installed to remove the smoke from the burning oil and the daytime heat. The watch room, just below the lantern room had an external gallery with an iron parapet, allowing for exterior access to the tower as a lookout and to the windows for cleaning. Once completed, the total cost of the Morris Island Lighthouse was $149,993.50 (an equivalent of more than $2 million today).

The Morris Island Lighthouse has two "sister" lighthouses, built on the same design for the tower, lantern room and gallery. The Bodie Island Lighthouse, Oregon Inlet, North Carolina, was built in 1872 and, like Morris Island, was painted in black-and-white bands. The second sister was the Currituck Lighthouse, built in 1875, at Corolla, North Carolina, on the Outer Banks. Unlike Morris Island and Bodie Island, Currituck was left unpainted.

Much like the Morris Island Lighthouse, Bodie Island had an earlier lighthouse, built in 1859. Though controlled by Union troops early in the war, Confederates overtook the lighthouse at night in 1861 and destroyed it by explosion.

The lighthouse was originally constructed twenty-seven hundred feet onshore. *Courtesy of the U.S. Coast Guard.*

The Morris Island Lighthouse was construcced using the same plans as the Bodie Island Lighthouse, built in 1872. The sister lighthouses were even paincted with similar black-and-white bands. *Courtesy of the Library of Congress.*

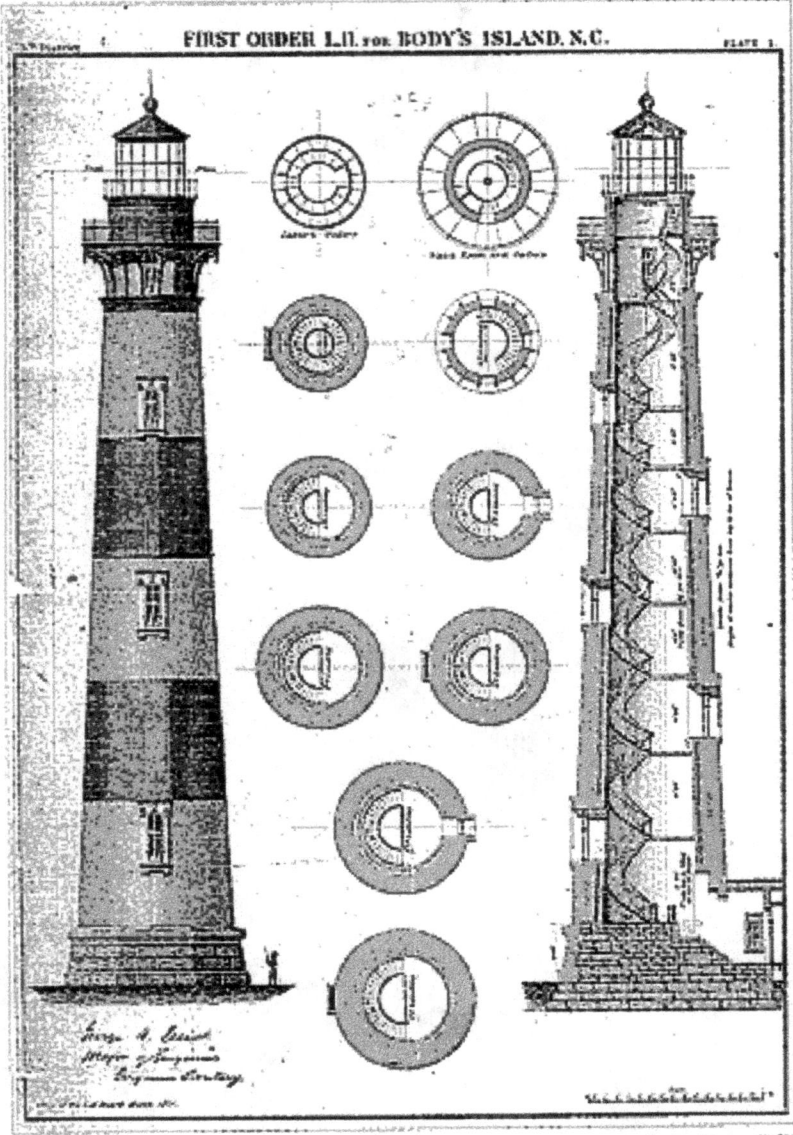

Plate I

Elevations and Sections

FIRST ORDER L.H. for BODY'S ISLAND, N.C.

The engineering plans for the Morris Island Lighthouse do not survive. However, the plans were identical to those for the Bodie Island Lighthouse, built several years earlier. *Courtesy of the Library of Congress.*

The Fort Ripley Shoal Lighthouse was located in eight feet of water in the inner harbor. The beacon was constructed on the site of a Civil War fortification named for Brigadier General C.S. Ripley. *Author's Collection.*

This photograph is of the "Old Rear Beacon," established in 1893 and discontinued just six years later. *Courtesy of Jim Booth.*

The Morris Island Lighthouse was first illuminated on October 1, 1876.

With work complete on the main lighthouse, attention was directed, once again, to the harbor beacons. In 1877, construction began on the most unusual light in the harbor system. Fort Ripley was an interior harbor fort built in 1862 on Middle Ground Shoal, located between the Battery and the northern shore on James Island. The fort was named for Brigadier General C.S. Ripley, the commander for Confederate forces on James Island and in St. Andrew's Parish.

The fort, built on piles over eight feet of water, was replaced by a lighthouse known as the Fort Ripley Shoal Lighthouse. This curious six-sided building, three stories tall, was placed atop wrought-iron screw pilings. The design allowed for a fifth-order Fresnel lens on top, fifty-one feet above mean high tide. The lens initially operated with a fixed white light that was changed in the twentieth century to a fixed red light. The structure also operated a fog bell, sounding every ten seconds.

The lighthouse was staffed with one keeper, living full time in the small lighthouse. The first keeper after completion in 1878 was Thomas Patrick O'Hagan. The lighthouse was stocked with a small boat suspended underneath, occasionally used by the keeper to row to town. Visitors would access the lighthouse by boat and then climb a ladder to the first level. The lighthouse was deactivated in 1932, though it remained in the harbor for some time.

Tour guides in the mid-nineteenth century frequently told a favorite joke while pointing to the Fort Ripley Lighthouse from the Battery. Visitors would be asked, "Did you know they raised all the vegetables they ate there?" Of course, they were all staring at a small structure suspended above water with no place to plant vegetables and no place for a roof garden. Inevitably, the visitors would ask, "How?" To which the pleased guide would respond, "They raised the vegetables in baskets from the boats that delivered them underneath to sell."

Life on the Island

The first keeper responsible for the new lighthouse was fifty-one-year-old G.R. Thompson, a Swedish immigrant. He was assisted by J.J. O'Hagan and John Ames. Thompson was single, but O'Hagan and Ames had their wives accompany them to this challenging new home. Ames also had two children, ages one and two, living on Morris Island.

The keeper, two assistants and their families lived in the three-story dwelling at the base of the tower. The lighthouse complex included fifteen buildings on the grounds. The head keeper had use of half of the house, upstairs and down. The two assistants shared the other half of the house, one living downstairs and the other living upstairs.

The keepers all worked together during the day, carrying oil in ten-gallon buckets up the nine flights of stairs and polishing the thousand-plus prisms of the lens and the lantern room windows every day. Each man was responsible for an eight-hour shift monitoring the operation of the light. The life of the keeper might seem romantic, but it was relentless and challenging work.

The two assistant keepers and the keepers for the Morris Island beacons were also responsible for collecting the bones of the many soldiers that would wash up as the shoreline eroded. The bones were collected daily in wooden barrels to be later buried again farther inland. This gruesome task continued through the 1930s.

In 1883, the U.S. Life-Saving Service, a predecessor agency to the U.S. Coast Guard, requested the use of the government property of the Civil War–era lighthouse to build a lifesaving station. The request was granted for a one-acre site to construct the living quarters and offices with an additional quarter-acre site to construct a boathouse.

The lifesaving complex was completed by the spring of 1885, now with the resources of two federal agencies to assist mariners. The boathouse was a forty-two- by eighteen-foot building housing a thousand-pound, self-bailing, self-righting surfboat. The boat, when needed, was pulled on a cart and launched into the surf. When necessary, the boat could be outfitted with a sail.

The lifesaving station was also equipped with a Lyle gun. This gun, resembling a cannon, was used to launch a strong hawser, a thick nautical rope, to distances up to six hundred yards. When a shipwreck was too close to shore or the seas were too rough to use the surfboat, the Lyle gun could fire the hawser to the stranded mariners. Once secured, the crew onshore could pull the men in distress to safety.

Left: This photograph, taken on June 10, 1914, is a good close-up of the tower and the keepers' dwelling. The dwelling was a fine work of craftsmanship, assembled entirely with wooden pegs. There was not a single nail used in the construction. *Courtesy of the U.S. Coast Guard.*

Below: The Morris Island Life-Saving Station, constructed in 1885, was built to assist mariners and boats in distress. This photograph depicts the boathouse and the surfboat used for rescue. This site later became the home to the Sheltering Arms orphanage, administered by Reverend A.E. Cornish, an Episcopal missionary. *Courtesy of the National Archives.*

In 1885, a German immigrant John Wieking, was assigned to the Morris Island Lighthouse as head keeper. He moved to the island with his wife Angiline and two children, Dora, five years old, and Annie, a year old. Even if he was prepared for the job as head keeper, he could not have anticipated the challenges that lay ahead in the next two years.

On August 25, 1885, a large hurricane hit Charleston. The community had not experienced a major storm in thirty-one years, leaving residents unprepared and inexperienced in anticipating and dealing with a large cyclone. This storm, with winds exceeding 125 miles per hour, left twenty-one people dead and millions of dollars in damage.

The storm completely destroyed the rear beacon on Morris Island and severely damaged three others. The keepers' house was damaged and the plank walks between the various buildings on the island were destroyed. Large sections of the seawall surrounding the lighthouse complex were overturned. The main lighthouse itself was not damaged.

The next year, another of nature's calamities hit Charleston. At 9:50 p.m., on August 31, 1886, one of the largest earthquakes ever to occur in the eastern United States sent its first shock wave. Most buildings in Charleston were damaged; many were destroyed. In the city, people rushed into the streets and "many fell on their knees and prayed aloud for mercy." Open areas such as Marion Square and Washington Square were crowded with people still in their night clothes, afraid to reenter any building. The aftershocks served to create further hysteria amongst the residents.

The effects of the earthquake were felt from the Sea Islands to Summerville. The lighthouse was damaged, as were many of the utility buildings and beacons. The Fresnel lens was tossed out of place and many prisms were cracked. The tower was cracked extensively in two places. The keeper's report to Washington noted, "The upper and most serious crack extends somewhat spirally almost through a full circumference of the tower."

The keeper also reported that the tower now appeared to list slightly seaward. Engineers from the U.S. Lighthouse Service and the U.S. Army Corps of Engineers were sent to Charleston to inspect the lighthouse tower. While they confirmed that the tower did indeed now list to the sea, they were confident that the stability of the foundation was not compromised.

Wieking was assisted by Angus Bennett, first assistant, and Francis Francott, second assistant. The normal operation of a seacoast light was demanding enough, but these men also faced the cleanup and repairs following the earthquake.

The keepers' house was full of activity. Though Francott was single, Bennett was accompanied by his wife and five children, ranging in ages from eleven to eight months old. The three families attempted to conduct a normal family life. Out of necessity, they raised or caught much of their food. They established vegetable gardens, though many items would not grow well in the sandy conditions. They raised chickens and pigs and enjoyed the plentiful seafood available in the salt waters.

Shrimp and crabs were plentiful. Oysters were readily available on the mud banks of the creeks behind Morris Island, though raking for oysters was a tricky business. Low tides, especially after storm tides, often exposed shells fired during the Civil War all over

Captain John Wieking, a German immigrant, was one of the longest tenured lightkeepers at the Morris Island Lighthouse. Shortly after accepting the post, he had to weather both the 1885 hurricane and the earthquake of 1886, the greatest threat to the lighthouse since the Civil War. *Courtesy of Mrs. Roulain Deveaux.*

Captain Wieking lived on Morris Island with his wife and children, Dora, Annie and John Jr. Dora later lived in Charleston and had six children. Annie married John R. Johnson, the son of Charleston haberdasher and photographer George W. Johnson. *Courtesy of Mrs. Roulain Deveaux.*

This photograph, taken by the Wieking family, shows a nest of turtle eggs found on the beach. Turtle eggs were a great delicacy and were eaten raw, cooked or used for baking. Charlestonians attest that the best cakes were made with turtle eggs! *Courtesy of Mrs. Roulain Deveaux.*

the area, many of them unexploded. The children were allowed to play at the lighthouse complex and on the beach, but were instructed to not venture inland alone.

The keepers went to town twice a month for supplies. Their children were always hoping that it was their turn to travel into the city.

The late 1880s were busy years for the Wieking and Bennett families. The Bennetts had three more children: Alfonso (1886), Eric (1887) and Leroy (1889). John Wieking and his wife had their third child, John, in 1889.

In the late 1880s, the lifesaving station moved to Sullivan's Island. Reverend Andrew Ernest Cornish, an Episcopal priest, purchased the land and buildings from the U.S. Life-Saving Service. After modifying the property, he moved his orphanage, Sheltering Arms, from James Island to Morris Island.

Like the keepers' families, Cornish tried to operate the orphanage with as much self-sufficiency as possible. The boys collected driftwood for firewood and the girls kept house. Cornish would meet produce boats at the docks to collect overripe fruit and produce that was not suitable for sale. He bought barrels of broken crackers and cookies from a Charleston bakery—a great treat for his charges and one they shared with the lightkeepers' children.

George Shierlock Sr. was a lightkeeper serving aboard a lightship at Frying Pan Shoals off the North Carolina coast. In 1886, Shierlock was found murdered in his stateroom, his throat cut. He left behind a son, George Jr. With no other living relatives, the U.S. Lighthouse Service delivered the boy to the Sheltering Arms orphanage on Morris Island.

This picture was taken by George W. Johnson, reclining in the center, using a cable shutter release. Johnson's son married the daughter of Captain Wieking, the Morris Island lightkeeper. The Charlestonians are depicted here during a visit to the Sheltering Arms orphanage. *Courtesy of Mrs. Faith Ferguson.*

While visiting the Sheltering Arms orphanage on Morris Island, guests take time out to ride the kids' pull cart on the beach. *Courtesy of Mrs. Faith Ferguson.*

The Sheltering Arms orphanage moved to Summerville, South Carolina, in 1908.

While the seafood available was plentiful, it was also monotonous. The keepers' families always looked forward to the fall migration of ducks. Each year, ducks would hit the lighthouse tower in the dark of night, the impact killing them and thus providing for the eager families at the lighthouse complex.

On one occasion, the Wieking and Bennett families were asleep and were awakened by a great commotion outside. They investigated the grounds and found a collection of ducks lying at the base of the lighthouse. Being the middle of the night, the ducks were gathered and left in the kitchen for cleaning in the morning. Later, the families were awakened again by an even greater commotion, this time inside the house. Running to the kitchen, it appeared that the ducks had been simply stunned by their collision and were not dead. They had regained consciousness and were flying all through the downstairs of the house!

The three keepers and families lived in close quarters and life was generally most congenial. On one occasion, however, John Wieking was pulling duty in the lantern room at night. An assistant keeper, a single man living in the quarters, entered the bedroom belonging to the Wieking daughters. He put chloroform over the face of one girl, presumably to molest the other. The other assistant keeper overheard the girl's screams and sounded an alarm bell, attracting Wieking's attention. The offending keeper, now scared of discovery, ran back to his quarters, barricaded himself inside and took his own life.

Wieking served on Morris Island for twenty-three years before retiring in 1908. He was relieved by Lewis H. Bringloe. Bringloe had two assistants, George Jackson and Albert Burns. Burns left the lighthouse service just before World War I. With the cost of the war, funds in the lighthouse service were tight. The lighthouse board offered Bringloe a choice between eliminating the second assistant position and receiving a long overdue pay increase himself or foregoing the increase and filling the position. He chose to fill the position. When hired, the second assistant received a wage of $600.00 per year and a ration allowance of $164.25.

George Shierlock Jr., the orphan of a lightkeeper, became a lightkeeper himself, accepting the position of assistant at Morris Island. He and his wife Catherine lived in the four-room apartment in the keepers' dwelling. Shierlock served with the lighthouse and, like his father, aboard the lightships operating out of Charleston Harbor.

In 1914, the U.S. Lighthouse Service appropriated $60,000 to purchase 3.66 acres of highland and four acres of marsh at the west end of Tradd Street to build a new lighthouse depot on the Ashley River. The new depot included a wharf for berthing lightships, a three-story brick building, a double-dwelling for keepers, a garage, blacksmith shop and an oil house. The depot was the home and headquarters for H.S. Beck, the superintendent of the sixth lighthouse district, which extended from New River Inlet, North Carolina, to Hillsboro Inlet, Florida.

In May 1915, a ferocious gale hit Charleston Harbor leaving thirty fishermen stranded on Morris Island. They were fishing the shipping channel in five boats, but could not weather the rapidly approaching storm. The keepers fed and clothed the men and provided shelter for two days until they could be safely picked up by a boat downtown.

George Shierlock Jr. was the son of a lightkeeper found murdered aboard a lightship off the North Carolina coast. George was sent to the Sheltering Arms orphanage on Morris Island and later became a keeper at the lighthouse. *Courtesy of Jim Booth.*

Bringloe served as the head keeper until 1930. In 1925, he was joined by William Hecker, a soldier stationed at Fort Moultrie for the previous fourteen years. In 1925, Hecker accepted the position as first assistant keeper. Under Bringloe, the Morris Island Lighthouse was an efficient operation generally receiving efficiency, neatness and conduct ratings of 100 percent when inspected by Superintendent Beck.

The same year Hecker was married. His wife, Ester Hecker, recalled her introduction to Morris Island. "I went as a bride in 1925. Not the first night we were married because it was storming, but the second. Before we left, we had six kids living with us."

Also serving at the lighthouse was Edward Vance Hewitt. He lived on the island with his wife Anna and five children. In 1925, the Hewitt kids were the only children on the island. They spent many days spearing flounder in the tidal pools on the outgoing tides and raking oysters from the long dock on the back side of Morris Island. The boys, Ed, Leon and Bennie, spent many days enjoying their ten-foot sailboat in Lighthouse Inlet.

The Morris Island Lighthouse was traditionally staffed with three to four keepers. During the Depression, the staff was reduced to two men. Hecker had been promoted to head keeper after the departure of Bringloe. His assistant was W.A. Davis. In 1933, Davis was transferred to Staten Island. Replacing him was Edward Lockwood Meyer, born and raised on nearby John's Island.

William and Ester Hecker lived on Morris Island with their six children: William, Alice, Ester, Charles, Jim and June. Mrs. Hecker noted, "I loved that place. If the tide hadn't washed the land away, we'd still be there." *Courtesy of Katherine Davis Craig.*

Mrs. Hecker recalled, "My daughter, Ester, was born in October 1929. There was a large storm so the doctor was called to the island. Our doctor lost an oar trying to row over [from Fort Johnson]. He had to turn back. His Dad was a doctor too and he finally got through. We nicknamed Ester the 'Storm Baby.'" *Courtesy of Katherine Davis Craig*

The lighthouse complex was connected to the wharf and island beacons by wooden walkways. This walkway extended to the back of the island, reaching the wharf on Lighthouse Inlet. *Courtesy of Katherine Davis Craig.*

Meyer lived in the keepers' house sharing space with the Hecker family. Meyer's younger children lived on the island, but his older children lived with relatives on John's Island so they would have access to high school.

The education of the keepers' children was dependent upon the number of children on the island. Charleston County regulations provided that any Sea Island with as many as five school-age children would be provided a teacher. In years with fewer children, they were schooled by their mothers. In years with at least five children, a teacher would be brought to the island, where he or she lived with the families from Monday to Friday, providing education for the students. One room in the keepers' dwelling was set up with desks and a blackboard.

Like most keepers before them, the Meyer family kept a vegetable garden on the island and raised their own livestock. They had a pet German shepherd named Wolf and a small black kitten.

Meyer owned a Model T Ford he kept on Folly Island. With a small staff, he decided to bring it to the island in 1934 for transportation from the lighthouse to the island's beacon lights. The Meyer children also drove the car all over the island. After a year, the old car quit operating and the family converted it to a chicken coop.

In one newspaper interview, Meyer's daughter Ellen recalled a storm surge in 1935 that swept over the island. The family's chickens, pigs and turkeys were all swept out to sea.

Every week, teacher Elma Bradham would travel by boat to Morris Island. She would teach the island's children during the week, living with them. On Friday, she would return to her home on John's Island for the weekend. *Courtesy of Katherine Davis Craig.*

Lightkeeper Ed Meyer moved his Model T Ford to Morris Island in 1934. Of course, it begs the question, "How do you move a car to an island with no road, bridge or ferry access?" The answer can be found in this photograph taken by Katherine Davis with her Brownie camera. The car was loaded onto three rowboats at Folly Island and carefully eased to Morris Island. *Courtesy of Katherine Davis Craig.*

Assistant W.A. Davis (left) and Captain William Hecker (right) were the last two lightkeepers to serve on Morris Island. They are pictured here with Hecker's dog Billy. They were ordered to evacuate the island in 1938 and the lighthouse was automated. *Courtesy of Katherine Davis Craig.*

This picture, taken by Katherine Davis, shows the long walkway leading to the lighthouse complex. These walkways were used to connect the various dwellings, beacons and the wharf for easy access. *Courtesy of Katherine Davis Craig.*

Families living on Morris Island raised their own chickens and pigs for food. Katherine Davis recalled, "We had all the fish, crabs, shrimp and clams we could eat. In the fall, we ate ducks and marsh hens. I would row the boat and Dad would shoot the marsh hens." This photograph is of Sarah Davis and her pet rooster. She does later reminisce that living on Morris Island was a "godsend." *Courtesy of Katherine Davis Craig.*

In 1935, Meyer was transferred to maintain the harbor beacons and Davis was brought back from Staten Island. From 1935 until the island was abandoned in 1938, Hecker and Davis were the last lightkeepers to serve on Morris Island.

With the staff cut back to two lightkeepers, Hecker rigged an alarm bell installed on the keepers' beds. If the light went out or the lantern mechanism malfunctioned, the bell would alert them during the night. This eliminated the need for someone always on watch at night in the tower.

However, in inclement weather, one keeper always manned the lantern room. When he could no longer see the beacon at the jetties, he telephoned the radio station at Fort Sumter to initiate a radio beacon to guide ships.

Ester Hecker often spoke of the lighthouse complex being haunted. She believed that several troubled spirits inhabited the lighthouse. Legend held that a keeper in the nineteenth century fell to his death from the tower's parapet. Another keeper at the turn of the century, in an unsolved mystery, was found in a supply closet in a building on the island with his throat cut. Then, of course, there was the assistant keeper that committed suicide after attempting to molest Wieking's daughter.

Even in the 1930s, life on Morris Island remained a challenge. Like Meyer before him, Davis had to find housing for his high school-age daughter. He rented a room for her with an elderly woman on Folly Island. Each morning she would catch a ride with a

In this photograph, the Hecker and Davis families take time out to enjoy the beach. *Courtesy of Katherine Davis Craig.*

DWELLING

STORE HOUSE

STORE HOUSE

OIL HOUSE

OFFICE

TOWER

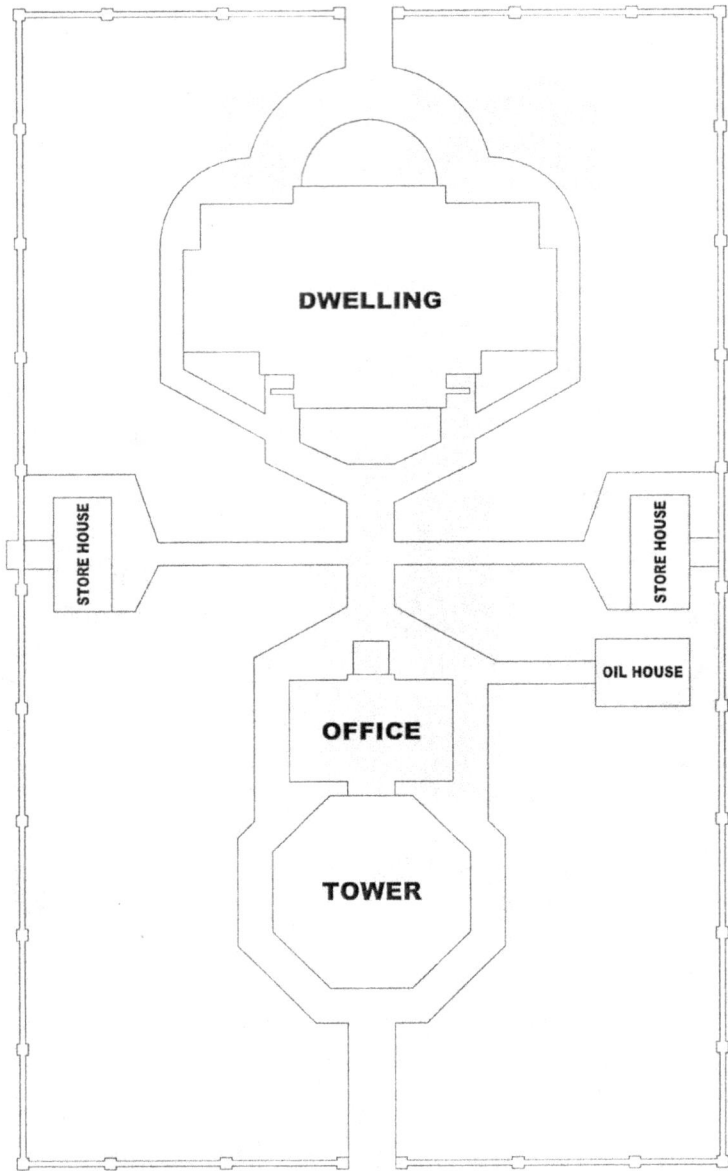

**SITE LAYOUT OF MORRIS ISLAND
LIGHTHOUSE FACILITY AS OF 1917**

SCALE: 1"=20'-0"

DRAWN BY: C. B. ARDIS
BERENYI INCORPORATED

The lighthouse complex included the tower, keeper's office, the keepers' dwelling, the oil house and two storehouses. A brick seawall enclosed the complex. *Courtesy of Save the Light.*

By the 1930s, lightkeepers no longer rowed into Charleston by boat to visit or for supplies. Lightkeepers Davis and Hecker maintained personal automobiles in a garage on Folly Island, a short boat ride away. *Courtesy of Katherine Davis Craig*

produce truck to attend school in Charleston. She would return to Morris Island on the weekends to be with her family.

There was no fresh water available on the island. The families captured rainwater in a cistern located in the bottom of the house. During dry spells, it was not unusual for the cistern to run dry, forcing the keepers to transport fresh water in kegs filled at Fort Johnson on James Island.

Davis and Hecker made bimonthly trips to Charleston for supplies. They would load the boat with cans of lard, twenty-pound sacks of flour and rice and cans of evaporated milk. They would also transport a hundred-pound block of ice. This would serve to refrigerate food as long as it would last. When it completely melted, the refrigeration was over.

The closest doctor was at Fort Johnson. Though not far in the distance, it was a rough boat ride away, usually in choppy sea. They never sought a doctor's help unless it was an emergency. Instead, the families relied on a collection of home remedies. Of course, castor oil was good for any ailment. Anyone complaining of a sore throat would quickly have it painted with iodine. Cobwebs were used to cover a cut. Survival on the island required recipes to make writing ink from berries, homemade dyes for clothes, potions to rid pests and a host of concoctions to make homemade soap.

Ester Hecker, when reminiscing about her time on the island said, "We got pretty lonesome but we went to town once or twice a month, so it wasn't so bad."

"Water at the Doorstep"

The Morris Island Lighthouse was originally constructed twenty-seven hundred feet onshore. Major Hains and the lighthouse board would have never fathomed the fate that would befall the new seacoast light.

After the Civil War, there were many trained engineers, Confederate and Union, who sought new careers. Just as Hains turned to the U.S. Lighthouse Service, Brigadier General Gillmore, the Union commander leading the siege of Charleston, offered his services to the Army Corps of Engineers. In no small irony, he was initially assigned to Charleston.

The shipping channel was always challenged by the silt that flowed from the Ashley and Cooper Rivers. This often filled in the deep-draft channels, leaving shallow depths endangering deep-draft ships at low tide. After the Civil War, the main channel was only twelve to thirteen feet deep at low tide, causing large ships to anchor at the mouth of the channel until the tide changed.

Gillmore designed a system of harbor jetties that, once in place, could keep a deep-draft channel scoured to acceptable depths. He theorized that the outflow of water could keep a deeper channel cut through, perhaps as deep as twenty-one feet.

The chamber of commerce in Charleston lobbied Congress for funds to construct the jetties as designed by Gillmore. The chamber was marketing Charleston as the "shortest, cheapest and most reliable route by which to send their [western grain growers] productions to European, South American and West Indian markets."

U.S. Senator M.C. Butler of South Carolina introduced legislation for the construction of the "National Jetties" in Charleston. The bill passed Congress, and in September 1878, a contract was awarded to a New York construction company based on its bid of twenty-one dollars per linear foot. In a strategic move, the northern firm also pledged to use South Carolina granite, railroads and labor for the massive undertaking.

Gillmore's design called for the installation of an "apron" of heavy logs and brush. On top of this "apron," three layers of large riprap granite stone would be installed. In December 1878, work began on the north jetty at Sullivan's Island, which started 1,800 feet east of the Bowman jetty. The south jetty started just 650 yards from Cummings Point on Morris Island.

In 1863, General Quincy A. Gillmore was given command of the Department of the South for the Union army and coordinated the siege of Charleston, 1863–1865. After the Civil War, he accepted a position with the U.S. Army Corps of Engineers and designed the Charleston jetties. *Author's Collection.*

The ambitious project took seventeen years to complete, finished in the summer of 1895. When finished, the north and south jetties extended more than fourteen thousand feet along the shipping channel. The final price tag for the project was $3,707,932.77.

The jetties' design worked and the main shipping channel was deepening. However, there was an unintended consequence. The jetties created new sand transport patterns and cut off the supply of sand to the shores of the adjacent islands. With the strong winter storm waves, both Morris Island and Sullivan's Island began rapidly eroding.

Two spur jetties were designed and installed on the north side of the jetties to halt the erosion on Sullivan's Island. Four spur jetties were designed as a similar solution on the south side to aid the Morris Island shoreline; however, Congress never funded the project. Morris Island began eroding at an average rate of twenty-five feet per year.

Initially, the lighthouse was so far inland that the erosion caused little concern. By the 1920s, the lighthouse keepers were taking notice as the erosion was accelerating. By 1930, official reports to the lighthouse board were sounding the alarm.

In a report on April 29, 1930, Charleston Superintendent H.L. Beck noted:

In this photograph, Captain Wieking and his brother are walking the Morris Island beach. By the late nineteenth century, the beach erosion was already progressing at a rapid rate. *Courtesy of Mrs. Roulain Deveaux.*

Erosion of the beach in front of the station is proceeding at an alarming rate. Fifteen months ago the high water mark was nine hundred feet from the station. Its distance now is only four hundred feet.

Beck recommended the construction of four "experimental groins" similar to those installed earlier in 1930 at the Hillsboro Inlet Lighthouse in Pompano Beach, Florida.

In a report filed on May 3, a lighthouse inspector suggested that the erosion might be ignored, and that due to a shifting of the harbor channel, "as a guiding light to Charleston, its usefulness is past. Traffic, coastwise, is well served by the lightships." K. Mathisen, master of the lightship *Mangrove*, disagreed with the assessment, offering, "This lighthouse is an important aid, particularly to vessels entering the harbor from the south, of which there is a considerable number." Captain J.P. Johnson, of the lightship *Cypress*, weighed in as well, agreeing that the Morris Island Lighthouse should be retained.

The deputy commissioner of the U.S. Lighthouse Service agreed with Beck's recommendation to install the groins. His report to the board pointed out:

The Sixth District Superintendent is considerably alarmed by the recent very rapid inroads. If it continues at the rate of the last fifteen months, the sea will be washing the yard enclosure.

By 1938, the high tides had washed away the walkways and the steps leading to the assistant keeper's apartment, destroyed the workhouse and damaged the wall surrounding the complex. *Courtesy of Katherine Davis Craig.*

Even by the early twentieth century, storm tides occasionally reached the lighthouse complex. Mrs. Hecker recalled, "We loved the island, but the waves were coming in my door." *Author's Collection.*

Mrs. Davis and her daughter Sarah pose on the wall surrounding the lighthouse complex. At high tides, Katherine Davis told of hearing the water lapping against the wall outside her bedroom. Despite the presence of the water at the doorstep, Captain Hecker wrote in his report on June 3, 1938, "There is no danger to us yet." *Courtesy of Katherine Davis Craig.*

The board approved the expenditure for the groins and they were completed by June 12, 1930.

In an inspection again at summer's end, it was obvious that the new groins were doing little to arrest the rate of erosion. Beck suggested to the board that should the tower be further threatened or the quarters uninhabitable, the service should consider erecting a skeleton tower at Fort Moultrie on Sullivan's Island. He recommended that the Morris Island Lighthouse and the dwelling be enclosed with a sheet pile cofferdam protected with riprap stone. The permit for the Fort Moultrie tower was secured but not acted upon.

Through the next six years, no corrective measures were initiated, but the continued erosion was carefully monitored. In January 1937, the lighthouse board agreed to retain the use of the Morris Island Lighthouse rather than pursue the Fort Moultrie option. They further announced that the time had arrived to install a cofferdam around the Morris Island tower for protection from the seas. Their letter to Beck stated:

> *This handsome tower forms a very valuable daymark on a coastline not too well provided with conspicuous landmarks and in a location and of a type which would not perhaps be equally served by the previously suggested skeleton tower on Sullivan's Island.*

On July 19, 1937, Beck filed a report to the lighthouse board outlining his plans:

Propose to remove the first order lens and install the automatic illuminating apparatus on the fourth order lens already on hand. Fourteen A-50 accumulators will be installed in the tower base. Seven will be connected and seven reserved for emergency. As soon as automatic equipment is installed, the keeper personnel will be reduced from two to one until the equipment is thoroughly tried out. Then all keepers will be discontinued and the light made entirely unwatched.

Head lightkeeper Hecker wrote to Beck on June 3, 1938, reviewing his problems with the advancing waters, noting:

The last high tide we were having has taken just about over half of the station yard. The steps going to the second assistant's quarters have been washed away…The walkway going into the tower has washed away…The workhouse has washed down…But there is no danger to us yet.

The lighthouse tower was now two-thirds surrounded by water at high tide.

After a storm in 1938, the lighthouse complex was damaged by the water surge. In this photograph, the keepers' privy is overturned. The moral to the story is that when the privy's overturned, it is time to leave the island! *Courtesy of Katherine Davis Craig.*

On June 14, the contract for the sheet pile and cofferdam was awarded. The plan called for piles to be driven in a complete interlocking circle, approximately sixty feet in diameter, extending to four feet above the ground. The cofferdam would then be filled with sand and capped with concrete.

On June 22, 1938, the lighthouse was converted to an acetylene-powered lens and automated. The first-order Fresnel lens was put in storage at the lighthouse depot on Tradd Street in Charleston. Hecker, Davis and their families were ordered to leave the island. Ester Hecker remarked:

> *When we first went, there was so much land you could barely see the water. When we left, the water was at the doorstep. But I loved that place. If the tide hadn't washed the land away, we'd still be there.*

Davis was transferred to another light station. Hecker was transferred to the lighthouse depot in Charleston and assigned responsibility for the buoys, lights and markers in Charleston Harbor until his retirement.

Beck decided to remove the dwellings at the lighthouse complex. He feared that, if allowed to wash away, the debris would surely create a hazard for mariners. Seizing the

By the summer of 1938, the lighthouse was on the shoreline. A careful investigation of this aerial photograph reveals the roof, already being disassembled by Muckenfuss and his workers, as the keepers' dwelling was dismantled and the wood salvaged. *Courtesy of Jim Booth.*

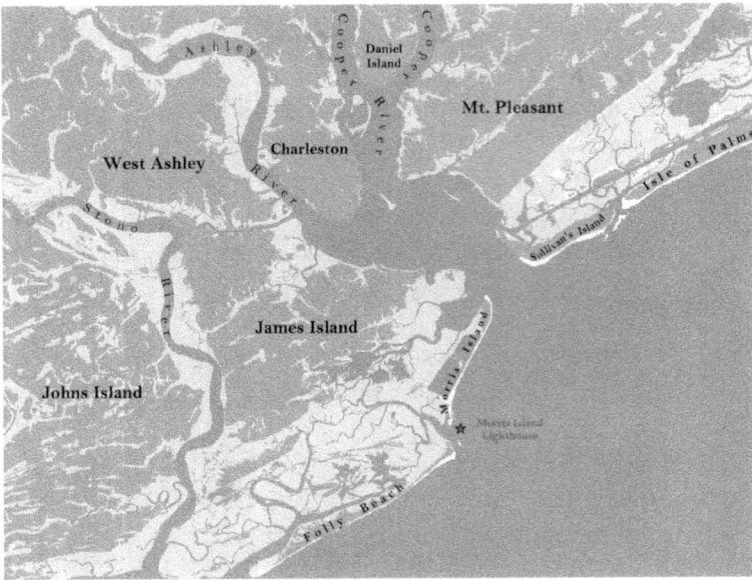

This map reveals the location of the Morris Island Lighthouse just offshore. From this viewpoint, it is easy to judge why the location on Morris Island was an effective guide for ships entering Charleston Harbor. *Courtesy of the Lowcountry Open Land Trust.*

opportunity, Dr. Richard Prentiss, a local physician, bought the dwellings for fifty-five dollars as government surplus property. He was a country doctor in Adams Run, twenty-eight miles from Charleston. Prentiss was well known for his courtesy care to the poor families in his area. He not only provided medical care, but he also bought groceries from Ohlandt's Grocery in Charleston at his own expense to provide for these indigent families.

Prentiss paid Mr. Muckenfuss and a crew of four workers to remove the keepers' dwelling. As they disassembled the house, they discovered the entire structure was constructed with pegs, not a single nail had been used. In addition to the obvious craftsmanship, the wood used was of great quality.

Starting with the roof, it took four weeks to carefully disassemble the dwelling. The wood was loaded onto a barge and taken to the Puckhaber dock at Secessionville on James Island for unloading. The second load was also shipped by barge, but to Yonges Island, unloaded and trucked to Edisto Island. Prentiss used the wood to construct two beach houses at Edisto Island. Unfortunately, some years later, the beach houses were destroyed during a storm and washed out to sea.

The only remnants of the keepers' house today are several support beams in Muckenfuss's house to support a second-floor bedroom. His daughter's home on James Island has a window frame from the dwelling installed in her home.

In 1863, General Gillmore failed to take Morris Island by force, yet after the war, he successfully destroyed the island with his jetties. In 1880, the Morris Island Lighthouse was built twenty-seven hundred feet onshore. By 1939, the lighthouse was in the surf. By 2000, the lighthouse was standing sixteen hundred feet offshore.

Lighthouse for Sale

The operation of the Morris Island Lighthouse required only a monthly visit to clean the windows and replace the acetylene gas cylinders. The fourth-order acetylene-powered light had six thousand candlepower and flashed four times every thirty seconds. Like its predecessor, the light was still visible for nineteen miles.

In 1939, the U.S. Lighthouse Service was merged with the U.S. Coast Guard as part of President Roosevelt's Reorganization Act. The active lightkeepers were given a choice of accepting military positions or continuing to serve as civilian employees.

In World War II, fearful of approach by German submarines, the light was darkened. The Coast Guard formed a division called the "Beach Patrol," whose mission was to patrol the shore, guarding against enemy incursion. The Morris Island Lighthouse was staffed by volunteers using the tower as a lookout for enemy ships or submarines. Submarine nets were installed in the nearby creeks and inlets.

The South Carolina coast was never attacked, but Folly Island was the site of much activity as naval aviators trained there, dropping live bombs on the northeast end of the island. These large, repeated concussions created several cracks in the concrete base poured around the lighthouse in 1938. The structural integrity of the tower itself did not appear to be compromised.

After World War II, the Coast Guard established a station on the northeast end of Folly Island, closest to the lighthouse. The station was the site for the Charleston LORAN, a long-range radio navigational guide. The station transmitted a fixed radio beacon that could be received as far as a hundred miles out to sea, guiding ships to the Charleston Harbor channel.

In a 1948 interview with the *Charleston Evening Post*, a Coast Guard spokesman noted, "There is little fear that the Atlantic will undermine the foundation of one of the oldest lighthouses on the U.S. coast." Tongue in cheek, he stated that the biggest threat to the lighthouse was the ducks and geese, plentiful on the coast, who would smash the glass in the lantern room while flying high speeds at night.

In 1953, Morris Island was considered as a site to establish a "colored beach." Still in the throes of segregation, separate black beaches were established along the Atlantic Coast for African Americans, as they were not allowed on the "white beaches." Communities such as Atlantic Beach in Horry County, nicknamed the Black Pearl, and

In this photograph, taken in the 1940s, the lighthouse is already surrounded by water. The cofferdam and concrete cap, installed in 1938, can be seen at the base of the tower. *Courtesy of Jim Booth.*

Mosquito Beach on James Island were examples of black beaches in South Carolina. After investigation by the local NAACP, it was determined that the waters off Morris Island were shark infested and not suitable for a recreational beach. The offer by the state was declined.

In October 1954, Hurricane Hazel grazed the Charleston coast, creating high winds and leaving a great storm surge in its wake. The lighthouse was not harmed, but the beach was littered with debris. C.E. McCants, a Charleston insurance executive, led a beachcombing party to Morris Island after the storm. On the beach, the beachcombers found a 150-year-old keel from a large ship, a cask of rosin, a Dutch sailor's cap, many floats and nets and hundreds of shot and shell fired during the Civil War.

In the 1950s, the main shipping channel continued to shift, rendering the position of the Morris Island Lighthouse obsolete. The decision was made to follow through on a long debated proposal to locate a lighthouse on Sullivan's Island. The Sullivan's Island Lighthouse was completed in 1962. It was constructed with concrete and steel and an aluminum exterior, triangular in shape, and was 163 feet tall. The lighthouse looked more like an air traffic control tower than a lighthouse. The new lighthouse had the distinction of being the only lighthouse with an elevator rather than the traditional spiral staircase.

Initially the light had 28 million candlepower, the brightest light in the Western Hemisphere. The light was visible twenty-six miles out to sea. The light generated such intense heat that the keepers feared a spontaneous fire in the lantern room. By 1963, the light was decreased in power to just more than a million candlepower.

Once the Sullivan's Island Lighthouse was in operation, the Morris Island Lighthouse was deactivated. Lieutenant Commander E.R. Tindle, with the Coast Guard headquarters in Washington, announced that there were no plans to dismantle the Morris Island Lighthouse, stating, "So long as she remains in reasonably good shape structurally, we will let her stand." Interestingly, the Coast Guard quickly reversed its position and allocated $20,000 for the destruction of the lighthouse. It was rumored that a Georgia congressman was interested in the bricks from the tower, though no one with the Coast Guard would confirm that report.

Captain Julian J. Shingle of the Charleston Coast Guard Station did confirm that he was notified of the plans to demolish the lighthouse and he was instructed to ship the lens and the acetylene components to a lighthouse in California. Charlestonians reacted with anger at the prospect of the loss of their beloved lighthouse. Petitions immediately began circulating through Charleston, intended for the South Carolina delegation to Congress. The Coast Guard responded by placing twelve- by four-foot signs at the lighthouse marked, "Danger, Keep Off. Tower in danger of collapse. Trespassers will be prosecuted."

U.S. Senator J. Strom Thurmond and Congressman L. Mendel Rivers both filed requests with the Coast Guard urging that the decision to demolish the historic icon be reconsidered. They appropriately noted that no engineering study had been conducted to determine the integrity of the tower. They further asserted that the lighthouse was not in danger of collapse. Rivers indicated that his office was receiving more than ten letters a day in protest since the Coast Guard announcement.

The Sullivan's Island Light, constructed in 1962, resembled an air traffic control tower more than a lighthouse. This curious structure was the only lighthouse in the country that used an elevator. *Courtesy of the U.S. Coast Guard.*

The Preservation Society of Charleston announced that it would seek ownership of the lighthouse. In a statement to the press, Mr. Morrison, president of the society, announced:

> *This eighty nine-year-old structure has long been a landmark to this historic city. If, after further consideration of your plan, it is determined that the Coast Guard cannot maintain ownership and responsibility of this historic structure, then we urge you to consider transferring title to our organization for the purpose of preserving this historic monument for our community.*

Shortly, the Coast Guard announced that the demolition would be suspended while a possible transfer of title to the Preservation Society was explored. A month later, the Preservation Society withdrew its proposal to accept title. Morrison announced:

> *The Society is not set up to acquire properties for preservation, but rather is designed to stimulate the interest of others in the acquisition and preservation of distinctive properties.*

With the Preservation Society now backing off, Congressman Rivers asked the National Park Service to accept the lighthouse, but he was turned down.

Fortunately, though, the Coast Guard did withdraw its plans to demolish the lighthouse and transfer the structure and property to the General Services Administration for disposal as surplus property. The GSA announced that there were no government agencies interested in the lighthouse and it would accept bids from private groups or citizens for the property. The advertised sale included title to the Morris Island Lighthouse, 421 acres of land underwater and 140 acres of dry land.

By September 1965, the GSA announced it had received twenty-three bids for the lighthouse package. The high bidder, at $3,303.03, was John Preston Richardson, operator of the Bayview Motel and Apartments in Mount Pleasant and a former ship chandler. Richardson had bid on the property without ever inspecting the lighthouse. He announced, "I couldn't be more thrilled. I've got plans to preserve it and maybe plant some oyster beds beside it." Richardson spoke of the possibility of establishing a campground and a maritime museum on the highland.

When Richardson finally did inspect the land and lighthouse, he remarked that he was impressed with the view but shocked at the disrepair of the lighthouse. He was now considerably less enthusiastic. He offered to donate the lighthouse and property to the city or the state if they would also agree to finally construct the spur jetties to protect Morris Island and prevent further erosion. Neither was interested. Four months later, Richardson announced that he would sell the lighthouse and the immediate five acres of land underwater.

Charleston realtor Fred Wichmann listed the property for sale, representing Richardson. Wichmann, the son of a former lightkeeper at Cape Romain, had been a competitor bidder to Richardson for the first sale. He announced, "It's not available as salvage. Mr. Richardson wants it to go to a buyer with adequate funds to repair and preserve it."

In September 1966, a group of local realtors, including Henry Yaschik and S.E. "Speedy" Felkel, purchased 820 acres of Morris Island from Captain Anton Petterson. This tract, which included 400 acres of highland, gave them title to all of Morris Island other than the tract owned by Richardson. A month later, Felkel bought the land and lighthouse from Richardson for $25,000.

Saved by Save the Light

Speedy Felkel owned the lighthouse for thirty years. He often spoke of plans to create a development and tourist site of Morris Island and the lighthouse. Felkel used the lighthouse as collateral for a loan and in 1996 forfeited title in a foreclosure action for $100,000 brought by Columbia businessman Paul Gunter. Gunter, not anxious to own a lighthouse in standing water, announced that he would offer it for sale.

James Island resident Barbara Schoch was inspired to action by the urge to preserve the lighthouse. After speaking to friends, she was encouraged to speak with Johnny Ohlandt, owner of nearby Black Island. Ohlandt had visited Morris Island as a child when his father took him fishing. He spent many afternoons playing with the lightkeepers' kids while his dad visited. Ohlandt frequently visited the lighthouse, tying his johnboat to the lighthouse base while he enjoyed another climb up the stairwell to the top.

Schoch and Ohlandt found no trouble in finding other interested James Island and Folly Beach residents to form the Morris Island Lighthouse Committee. In a "Letter to the Editor" Schoch wrote:

> Lighthouses have always played an important role in our maritime history while symbolizing safety, security, heroism and faithfulness. Please help us remain faithful to ourselves by preserving this important piece of our past, present and future.

The public did respond in a big way. Thousands of citizens signed petitions urging that the Charleston County Parks and Recreation Commission acquire the lighthouse. The commission entertained the idea and consulted with the State of South Carolina over ownership. The state claimed that since the lighthouse land was underwater, the property and the lighthouse were now owned by the state. A judge rejected that argument, indicating that the state should have made that claim at the foreclosure action a year earlier. The state attorney general's office indicated that it would respond to the ruling with a suit to clarify title.

Time passed and the suit never materialized. During the time state and local agencies engaged in an endless debate over the future of the lighthouse, another realtor was expressing interest in the historic property.

Johnny Ohlandt was the closest thing to a modern-day keeper for the Morris Island Lighthouse. A noted conservationist and owner of nearby Black Island, Ohlandt was once described as having a Lowcountry brogue "as thick as pluff mud!" *Courtesy of Save the Light.*

The lighthouse committee of citizens became exasperated over the delays, and in November 1998, incorporated as Save the Light, Inc. The simple mission of the group is to "save and preserve the Morris Island Lighthouse for the People of South Carolina." In February 1999, Save the Light purchased the Morris Island Lighthouse for $75,000 from Gunter. Local artist Jim Booth and Charleston businessman Robert New personally guaranteed the loan for Save the Light until the money could be raised, which was accomplished in short order.

John F. Hassell III, president of the Maritime Association, in a letter to the editor of the *Post and Courier* wrote:

> *Saving the Morris Island Lighthouse is symbolic of what's great about America. A group of citizens recognize a need, and they get together and do something about it. In the case at hand, the need is to acquire and stabilize a structure, which, more than anything else, attests to our heritage as a seafaring community…The Maritime Association of the Port of Charleston has made a financial contribution to Save The Light. We congratulate its organization on the acquisition of the lighthouse and thank them for their vision.*

In April 1999, the lighthouse found a home when it was annexed by the City of Folly Beach. Folly Beach Mayor Vernon Knox stated, "We're just proud to have it in the city. We felt very honored."

Save the Light was successful in its fundraising efforts with donations coming in from as far away as Switzerland. The group focused on elevating the public's consciousness of the plight of the lighthouse with bumper stickers and a website.

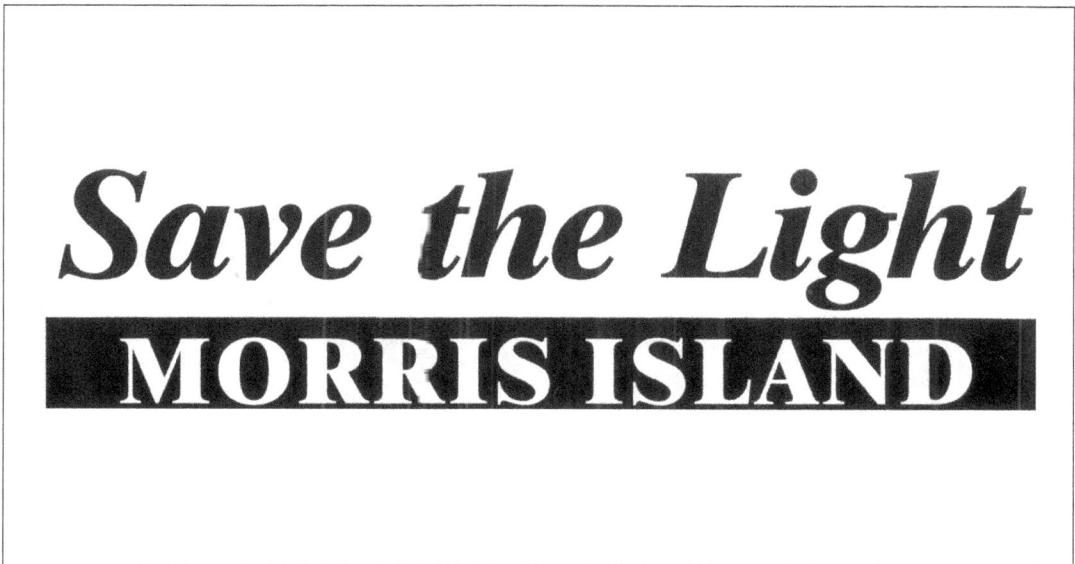

Save the Light initiated an effective awareness campaign with a simple bumper sticker. Many cars throughout the Lowcountry could be seen sporting the sticker and urging their fellow residents to support the efforts to save the Morris Island Lighthouse. *Courtesy of Save the Light.*

Charleston artist Jim Booth painted this scene of the Morris Island Lighthouse, entitled "First Light." He donated prints of this painting to Save the Light for use as a fundraiser for the stabilization project. *Courtesy of Save the Light.*

In 2001, South Carolina began offering a Morris Island Lighthouse license plate. The attractive and colorful plate was immediately a big hit with state motorists. A portion of the cost for the plate goes toward the preservation of the lighthouse. *Courtesy of Save the Light.*

On July 13, 2003, the U.S. Post Office issued a set of four stamps—the Southeastern Lighthouse series. The four lights selected were the Old Cape Henry Lighthouse in Virginia, the Cape Lookout Lighthouse at Tybee Island, Georgia, the Hillsboro Inlet Lighthouse in Florida and the Morris Island Lighthouse. *Courtesy of Save the Light.*

Above: Chairman Richard Beck and board member Paula Hinton, seen flanking the Morris Island facsimile, represented Save the Light at the First Day of Issue Ceremonies at Tybee Island. *Courtesy of Save the Light.*

Left: In 2002, Korean artist Kim Sooja used the Morris Island Lighthouse to create a Spoleto exhibit, "A Lighthouse Woman." Sooja "painted" the lighthouse in computer synchronized colors using lights at the base and in the lantern room. *Courtesy of Richard L. Beck, DMD.*

State of South Carolina
Proclamation
by
Governor Jim Hodges

WHEREAS, decommissioned in 1962, the Morris Island Lighthouse served the citizens of South Carolina for nearly three centuries, providing light to ensure maritime safety in Charleston Harbor; and

WHEREAS, the Morris Island Lighthouse is a testament to the rich history of Morris Island and the Palmetto State, providing a visible and tangible record of centuries of maritime industry; and

WHEREAS, tragically, the future of the Morris Island Lighthouse is threatened by years of neglect, vandalism, and the effects of the environment on the foundation, brickwork, and ironwork; and

WHEREAS, on December 13, 2000, the State of South Carolina will accept title to the Morris Island Lighthouse, which will then be leased to Save the Light for 99 years; and

WHEREAS, as a grassroots organization dedicated to the preservation of the history of the Palmetto State, Save the Light will work to raise funds and coordinate preservation and maintenance of the Morris Island Lighthouse for the enjoyment of residents and visitors now and in the future.

NOW, THEREFORE, I, Jim Hodges, Governor of the Great State of South Carolina, do hereby proclaim December 13, 2000, as

MORRIS ISLAND LIGHTHOUSE DAY

throughout the state and encourage all South Carolinians to recognize the importance of preserving this landmark to the rich history of the Palmetto State.

Jim Hodges
Governor
State of South Carolina

South Carolina Governor Jim Hodges declared December 13, 2000, as Morris Island Lighthouse Day, honoring the state's purchase of the historic icon from Save the Light for one dollar. The proclamation recognized the Morris Island Lighthouse as "a testament to the rich history of Morris Island and the Palmetto State, providing a visible and tangible record of centuries of maritime industry." *Courtesy of Save the Light.*

One early study of the stability of the lighthouse was inconclusive. The U.S. Army Corps of Engineers expressed interest in the project to save the lighthouse with both expertise and funding, but the ownership of the lighthouse would have to be with a state or local governmental agency. The federal charter of the U.S. Army Corps of Engineers does not allow the corps to work directly with Save the Light or any private group. The Army Corps of Engineers may work only on government-owned property or projects. Save the Light initiated a lobbying effort, asking the South Carolina Department of Natural Resources to accept title to the historic property.

On November 2, 1999, the *Post and Courier* offered an editorial stating:

> *Save The Light took charge of efforts to save the 123-year-old lighthouse, a nationally recognized landmark, when public agencies wouldn't. It has done a magnificent job: It purchased the lighthouse from the owner, sustained the initial purchase price, and initial engineering studies have been completed...The level of public support generated for its preservation underscores the importance of the historic Morris Island Lighthouse to the community. The campaign for its preservation now needs the assistance of the state to move to the next stage.*

Save the Light was directed to the Heritage Trust program, a program within the South Carolina Department of Natural Resources. The act establishing the Heritage Trust program entrusted it with the responsibility for the preservation of the important "natural areas" and "cultural areas" of the state. In the Heritage Trust Act, a "cultural area or feature" is defined as an

> *outstanding example of our historical or archaeological heritage and a site of special historic interest or containing outstanding remnants of the way of life and significant events of the past.*

In February 2000, the board of directors of the Heritage Trust recognized the Morris Island Lighthouse as one of the top one hundred cultural sites in the state of South Carolina and forwarded its unanimous recommendation to the DNR board to acquire the lighthouse from Save the Light. A mutually acceptable transfer was negotiated with the Heritage Trust Program Board. On April 21, 2000, the board of directors for the South Carolina Department of Natural Resources unanimously voted to accept title to the Morris Island Lighthouse.

After approval by the state budget and control board, the State of South Carolina accepted title to the Morris Island Lighthouse on December 13, 2000, in a ceremony at the Folly Beach City Hall. At the same ceremony, the state leased the lighthouse to Save the Light for ninety-nine years to coordinate the fundraising and preservation.

Preserving the
Old Charleston Light

There has been a concern for a half century that the foundation of the Morris Island Lighthouse would fail and the tower would collapse into the harbor. The Coast Guard first expressed this concern in 1963, though this "fear" was likely politically motivated to create public agreement that the lighthouse should be razed.

The lighthouse lens and tower were damaged in the 1886 earthquake. It is unknown if the structural integrity of the lighthouse was compromised, though the engineers did agree that it was listing seaward just slightly. The concussions of the navy bombing practice did produce some cracks in the concrete cap at the base, but, again, any real damage to the foundation is unknown.

A catastrophic failure and collapse of a lighthouse is not without precedent. Three small, brick lighthouses, called the "Three Sisters of Nanset," were constructed in 1839. By 1892, all three had fallen into the sea.

The Cape Henlopen Lighthouse was constructed on a large dune on the Delaware coast between 1765 and 1767. By the early twentieth century, the cape began to rapidly erode. The dune supporting the lighthouse was undermined and the lighthouse was abandoned in September 1924. Finally, on April 13, 1926, the lighthouse collapsed and fell into the sea.

Like the Morris Island Lighthouse, there are a number of lighthouses under threat due to erosion. The Montauk Point Lighthouse, in Montauk, New York, is within fifty feet of the cliff's edge. The Sand Island Lighthouse, near Dauphin Island, Alabama, was built on the same plans as the Morris Island Lighthouse in 1873. Sand Island was more than four hundred acres in the nineteenth century, but has now been reduced to less than one acre.

Certainly, one of the most celebrated lighthouse rescues was the moving of the Cape Hatteras Light 2,070 feet inland in 1999–2000. This project, however, created a "move it or lose it" philosophy that is not only practical, but also possible in many other situations.

In a persuasive article in the January 1991 issue of the *Journal of the American Shore and Beach Preservation Association*, two scientists celebrate the durability of the Morris

The Cape Henlopen Light, built between 1765 and 1767, in Delaware Bay was the victim of shifting sands at the cape. The beachfront was eroding an average of twenty-three feet a year in the nineteenth century. By the 1920s, the lighthouse was in danger of being undermined. It was abandoned on September 30, 1924. This photograph was taken just three days before the lighthouse collapsed into the bay. *Courtesy of the Delaware State Archives.*

The Montauk Lighthouse was first illuminated in 1797, making it the oldest lighthouse in New York and the fourth-oldest active lighthouse in the United States. In 1699, legend holds that Captain Kidd buried his treasure in two ponds at Montauk Point, today called the "Money Ponds," located near the footprint of the lighthouse. The severe erosion of the cliff has now endangered the lighthouse. In 2006, the U.S. Army Corps of Engineers announced plans to construct a seawall to protect the lighthouse. This drew sharp criticism from local surfers and area environmentalists claiming that the proposed work would ruin a "world-renowned surf break" and could accelerate erosion at other Long Island beaches. To date, the standoff has not been resolved. *Author's Collection.*

The Sand Island Lighthouse was built in 1873, on similar plans as the Morris Island Lighthouse. In another similarity, Sand Island is under threat by the severe erosion of the island offshore from Dauphin Island, Alabama. The town of Dauphin Island accepted title to the lighthouse from the federal government. Like Save the Light, the Alabama Lighthouse Foundation is currently raising money for the stabilization and preservation effort. *Author's Collection.*

Island Lighthouse in its present location. Authors Stephen Leatherman and Jakob Moller state:

> *The full range of possible options for historic lighthouses in the face of pervasive erosion is well demonstrated by the durability of the Morris Island Lighthouse. This outcome contrasts strongly with the perceived need to move the Cape Hatteras Lighthouse. The notion of "move it or lose it" is certainly not applicable everywhere. Its [Morris Island Lighthouse] present position graphically illustrates the process of coastal land loss and the rapidity at which erosion can occur. The history and present situation of the Morris Island Lighthouse can provide an invaluable educational lesson that could well be compromised if the decision had been to move it landward to another location.*

In July 1999, divers working with the U.S. Army Corps of Engineers tried to inspect the submerged foundation, but could not get past massive slabs of concrete poured around the lighthouse in 1938. The report from the Sheridan Corporation, a Charleston engineering firm, reported that the exposed pilings are greatly deteriorated, as one would suspect. Pilings that are exposed will be compromised. Since the pilings under the lighthouse could not be inspected, the Sheridan report concludes by noting,

Consulting engineer Carroll Crowther worked with Save the Light to make soil boring of the area around the lighthouse as various stabilization plans were considered. *Courtesy of Save the Light.*

International Chimney Corporation, an engineering firm out of New York, has deep experience with industrial chimneys and smokestacks; historic building and monument restoration and relocation; and lighthouse restoration and relocation. It was contracted to examine the foundation piles of the lighthouse. *Courtesy of Save the Light.*

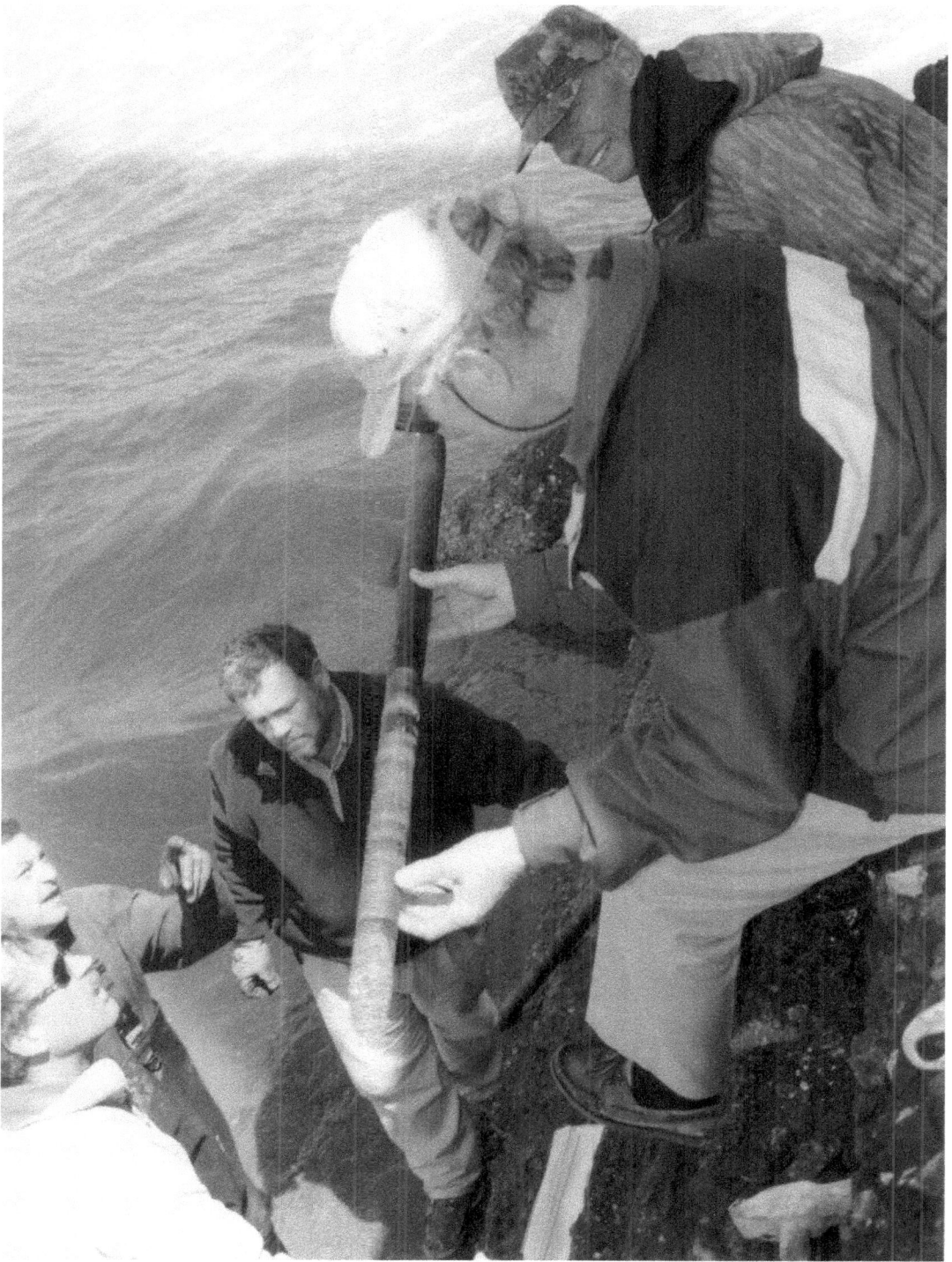

Core samples were taken of the wooden piles supporting the lighthouse. Exterior piles on the seaward side of the lighthouse were damaged by wood borers and deteriorated. However, piles on the north and west side of the lighthouse, still covered by sand, were in good shape. In this photograph Save the Light board members Al Hitchcock and Johnny Ohlandt inspect a sample pulled from the west side of the foundation. *Courtesy of Save the Light.*

The signing ceremony for the stabilization work on the lighthouse. Pictured are (left to right, standing) Folly Beach Mayor Carl Beckham Jr., U.S. Senator Lindsey Graham, Save the Light Board Chairman Richard Beck, U.S. Congressman Henry Brown, (left to right, seated) Lieutenant Colonel Edward R. Fleming (commander, Charleston district of the U.S. Army Corps of Engineers) and South Carolina Budget and Control Board Executive Director Frank Fusco. *Courtesy of South Carolina Budget and Control Board.*

Save the Light Board Member Al Hitchcock grants an interview about the stabilization work getting underway at the Morris Island Lighthouse in 2007. *Courtesy of Save the Light.*

Taylor Brothers Construction, a marine contractor from North Carolina, prepares the lighthouse site for installation of the sheet pile cofferdam. The strong seas at the harbor channel made the use of a jack-up barge necessary for crane operation. The first task was to remove the concrete debris from the previous efforts to save the lighthouse. *Courtesy of Save the Light.*

With the sheet pile in place, the next phase of work will place large riprap stone around the outside of the cofferdam. *Courtesy of Save the Light.*

The Morris Island Lighthouse was originally painted in bands of black and white. Over the many years that the tower has not been painted, the black paint, absorbing heat and sunlight, has dissipated, revealing the red brick underneath. Many people now mistakenly think the lighthouse was painted red and white. *Courtesy of Richard L. Beck, DMD.*

At low tide, the lighthouse stands dry at the base, allowing many curious boaters the opportunity to walk around the site. However, those not familiar with the harbor waters often find that when the tide turns it is easy to get stranded and separated from their boats. *Courtesy of Richard L. Beck, DMD.*

This photograph of the lighthouse base affords a great view of the rusted remnants of the 1938 cofferdam installed around the lighthouse. Above the door is a vacant space where the keystone proudly declared the date of construction as 1876 until it was stolen by vandals. The entrance has now been secured and the public may no longer enter the inside of the tower. *Courtesy of Richard L. Beck, DMD.*

The iron spiral staircase is a beautiful work of art and an incredible engineering achievement. The "floating staircase" rises the nine flights of the interior and is not secured to nor supported by the walls. It is only attached at the floor and the top. *Courtesy of Richard L. Beck, DMD.*

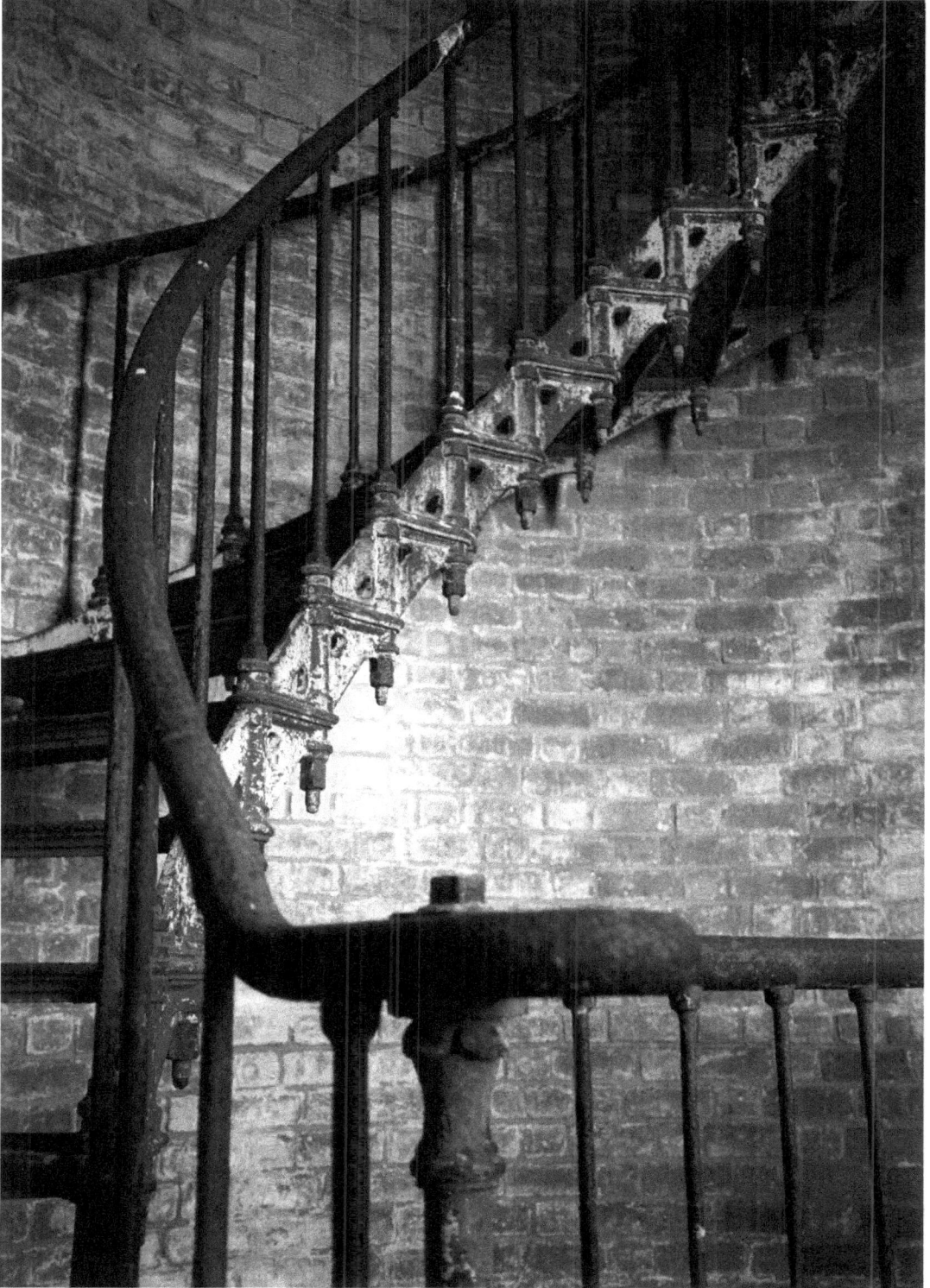

The ironwork needs attention but is generally in good shape. The sea air has not been kind to the extensive ironwork, which has been neglected since 1938. *Courtesy of Richard L. Beck, DMD.*

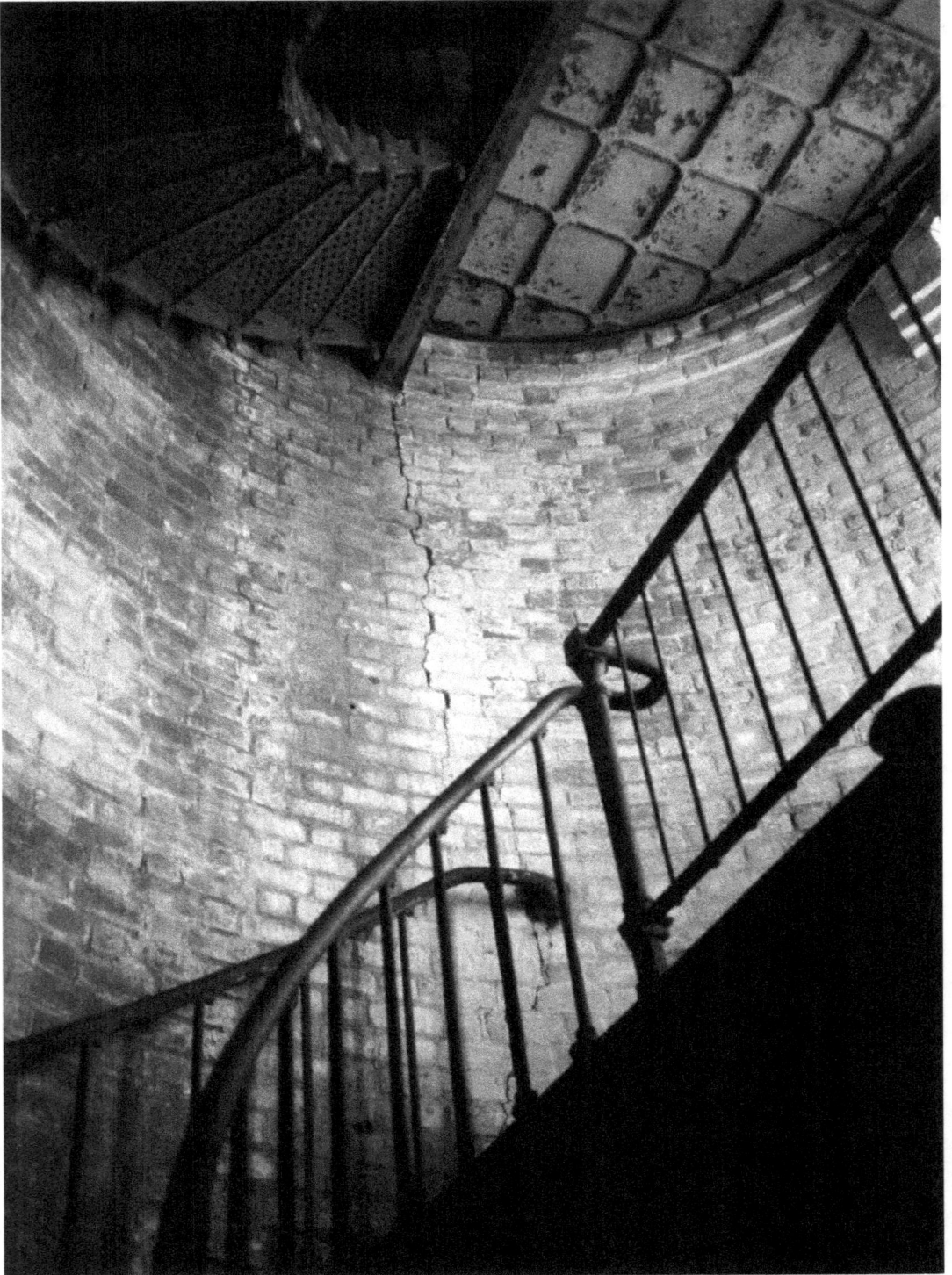

The interior and exterior walls betray signs of stress. Without current coats of paint or whitewash, the bricks have collected moisture that compromises their long-term condition. Also, the mortar needs to be repointed, a process of removing deteriorated mortar from the joints and replacing it with new mortar. Ultimately, painting the tower again will stabilize the brickwork. *Courtesy of Richard L. Beck, DMD.*

This photograph shows the decorative lights in the floor of the lantern room. Most of the glass is now missing, the victim of neglect, vandals and treasure seekers. *Courtesy of Richard L. Beck, DMD.*

This picture is of one of the decorative iron pendants on the lower edge of the parapet. The top of the lighthouse affords spectacular views of the surrounding ocean. *Courtesy of Richard L. Beck, DMD.*

This view from the lighthouse lantern room offers a beautiful view of the east end of Folly Island. The railing around the external gallery is in poor shape and needs to be replaced. The roof of the lighthouse is made of heavy-gauge copper and is in good shape. *Courtesy of Richard L. Beck, DMD.*

"The condition of the majority of the lighthouse foundation is unknown and subject to speculation."

Working with International Chimney Corporation in April 2001, core samples were taken of the pilings supporting the lighthouse foundation. The study revealed that a number of the pilings are exposed to the sea and have been damaged by shipworms.

After several years of study and consulting with the U.S. Army Corps of Engineers, work got underway in 2007 to stabilize the lighthouse foundation. The project has four phases: 1) Steel sheet piles are to be installed in the sand to form a cofferdam around the lighthouse; 2) Large riprap stones will be placed around the outside of the cofferdam to prevent further erosion; 3) A high-pressure grout will be injected below the lighthouse to reinforce and protect the original wood piles installed in 1873–74; and 4) a concrete cap will be installed inside the cofferdam.

After the foundation is stabilized and further funds are raised, attention will then be directed to the lighthouse tower including the brickwork, the ironwork and the lantern room. While there are no plans to open the lighthouse to the public, the historic Morris Island Lighthouse will continue to stand as a welcomed daymark for Charleston mariners.

Lightkeepers
Stationed on Morris Island

Lightkeeper	Years of Service
Ames, John	1876–1883
Bennett, Angus	1883–1903
Bringloe, Lewis H.	1908–1930
Bringloe, Richard	1858
Burns, Albert	1908
Burns, Edward	1887–1892
Calhoun, John	1806
Collins, Peter	1880–1881
Conklin, Henry	1876
Conklin, Jimmy	1875–1876
Davis, W.A.	1920s & 1930s
Dudley, Gilbert	1858
Ferrell, Ernest	1884
Francott, Francis	1883
Harm, William A.	1870
Hecker, William	1925–1938
Hewitt, Edward V.	1920s
Holmes, William	1858
Howard, John	1881–1883
Jackson, George	1910s
Jacobson, Ludwig	1906–1908
Jones, Thomas	1883–1884
Kearny, James	1858
Leavy, Martin	1878–1881
Lowridge, William	1860

Lightkeeper	Years of Service
Maniard, _____	1906–1907
Masindun, James	1873–1874
Mellichamp, St. Lo, I	Late 1700s
Mellichamp, St. Lo, II	1830–1856
Mellichamp, William A.	1858–1860
Meyer, Edward L.	1933–1935
Middleton, P.F.	1858
O'Hagan, John J.	1876–1880
O'Hagan, Thomas	1878–1887
Pepper, Phillip	1881
Player, Charles	1875–1876
Player, William	1874–1875
Read, William	1858
Rowell, Martin	1903–1906
Shierlock, George	1917–?
Sisson, Carl	1907–1908
Skillin, James	1858–1860; 1870–1873
Slavich, Matthew	1892–1894
Smith, C.K.	1866
Stonebridge, Richard	1884, 1887–1891
Svendsen, _____	1891–1896
Svendsen, Carl	1903–1908
Swann, Jessie	1902–1904
Thelning, Victor	1901–1902
Thompson, Gustavus R.	1878–1885
Wieking, John	1885–1908
Wilkinson, More	1884–1886
Wood, George	1850–1860
Wood, William	1860
Wragg, John	1881
Young, James	1882–1883

Note: This list, though incomplete, was compiled using the surviving historic reports and letters. Without a doubt, there were many more men to serve on Morris Island than are listed here.

Bibliography

Baldwin, William. "Carolina Lights." *South Carolina Wildlife* (March 1997).

Bostick, Douglas. *The Morris Island Lighthouse: Past, Present and Future.* Charleston, SC: Save the Light, 2000.

———. "The Revenge of General Gillmore." *The Journal* 11 (April 2002).

———. *Secession to Siege.* Charleston, SC: Joggling Board Press, 2004.

Burroughs, George. Letter to Admiral W.B. Shubrick, Chairman of the Lighthouse Board, December 7, 1869. Washington, D.C.

———. Letter to Admiral W.B. Shubrick, Chairman of the Lighthouse Board, December 11, 1869. Washington, D.C.

———. Letter to Admiral W.B. Shubrick, Chairman of the Lighthouse Board, December 16, 1869. Washington, D.C.

Burton, E. Milby. *Siege of Charleston.* Columbia: University of South Carolina Press, 1970.

"Ceding Title of the Lighthouse on Middle Bay Island to the United States." In *Statutes at Large of South Carolina.* Vol. V. 1790.

"Ceremony Transferring Title to the Morris Island Lighthouse." Unpublished program, December 13, 2000.

Chamberlain, David. "Middle Bay Light." *Charleston Magazine* (January 1977).

Charleston County Library, South Carolina Room, clipping files.

Charleston Mercury, December 20, 1861.

Charleston Yearbook. Charleston, SC: News and Courier Book Presses, 1883.

Conner, Sallie E. "Lighthouse Sparks Special Memories." *The Post and Courier*, August 4, 1985.

Cooper, Thomas, MD, LLD. *Statutes at Large of South Carolina.* Columbia, SC: A.S. Johnston, 1939.

Fraser, Walter J., Jr. *Charleston! Charleston!: The History of a Southern City.* Columbia: University of South Carolina Press, 1989.

Gadsden Family Papers. South Carolina Historical Society.

Hains, P.C. Letter to Joseph Henry, Chairman of the Lighthouse Board, November 10, 1873. Washington, D.C.

———. Letter to Professor Joseph Henry, Chairman of the Lighthouse Board, December 18, 1873. Washington, D.C.

————. Letter to Professor Joseph Henry, Chairman of the Lighthouse Board, December 29, 1873. Washington, D.C.

————. Letter to Professor Joseph Henry, Chairman of the Lighthouse Board, March 18, 1874. Washington, D.C.

Hains, Peter Conover file, Save the Light.

Harley, John B. Letter to Rear Admiral John Rogers, Chairman of the Lighthouse Board, June 20, 1878. Washington, D.C.

Hawes, Jennifer Berry. "Living On Top of the World." *Post and Courier.* November 24, 1999.

Historic Lightstation Information – South Carolina. United States Coast Guard. www.uscg.mil/history/WEBLIGHTHOUSES/LHSC.html.

History file, Save the Light.

History of the Charleston Main Light. Unpublished manuscript.

Jenkins, Thornton A. Letter to Commander B.N. Westcott, Lighthouse Inspector. November 23, 1869.

King, Brian. "Up for Grabs: Light, Land, Water." *News and Courier.* August 19, 1965.

Kirshner, Ralph. *The Class of 1861: Custer, Ames and Their Classmates after West Point.* Carbondale: Southern Illinois University Press, 1999.

Lighthouse and Lighthouse Keepers, South Carolina Historical Society.

"Lighthouse Deeds and Contracts, 1790–1853." National Archives.

"Lighthouse Woman." *Post and Courier,* May 11, 2002.

Mellichamp, Edward Henry, IV. *The Mellichamp Family History.* Columbia: R.L. Bryan Company, 1999.

Morris Island Lighthouse, Nomination for the National Register of Historic Places, 1984.

Nichols, Christopher. C. "An Examination of Shoreline, Barrier Ridge, and Cultural Change on Morris Island, SC." Unpublished paper. College of Charleston, 2000.

Nielsen, J.V., Jr. "Victorious Sea Marching on Morris Island, Drives Out Lightkeepers." *News and Courier,* June 5, 1938.

Peterson, Bo. "Keeping the Sea at Bay." *Post and Courier,* November 16, 2007.

"Plat of the Charleston Light Station." December 19, 1917.

Save the Light newsletters, 2000–01.

Shubrick, W.B. Letter to Major C. Burroughs, Lighthouse Engineer. December 6, 1869.

————. Letter to Major C. Burroughs, Lighthouse Engineer. December 20, 1869.

Simons, Katherine Drayton. *Stories of Charleston Harbor.* Columbia, SC: State Company, 1930.

"Specifications for Protecting Foundation of Charleston Lighthouse." June 10, 1938.

"Statement of Appropriations". United States Lighthouse Board. March 4, 1789 to June 30, 1882.

United States. Bureau of Lighthouse, Department of the Treasury. *Lighthouse Letters, 1 October 1800; 27 September 1809; 29 January 1798–30 September 1802.*

Wise, Stephen R. *Gate of Hell: Campaign for Charleston Harbor, 1863.* Columbia: University of South Carolina, 1994.

About the Author

Doug Bostick is an eighth-generation South Carolinian with ancestors dating back to Colonial America. A gifted storyteller and historian, he is the author of five books: *Secession to Siege 1860/1865*, *On the Eve of the Charleston Renaissance*, *Memorializing Robert E. Lee*, *The Boathouse: Tales and Recipes From a Southern Kitchen* and *Sunken Plantations: The Santee Cooper Project*.

Bostick, a former executive director of Save the Light, is a graduate of the College of Charleston and earned a master's degree from the University of South Carolina.

Visit us at
www.historypress.net

www.ingramcontent.com/pod-product-compliance
Lightning Source LLC
Chambersburg PA
CBHW050615110426
42813CB00008B/2565